ALICE MARRIOTT
REMEMBERED

ALICE MARRIOTT
REMEMBERED

Edited and with an Introduction and Annotations
by

CHARLOTTE WHALEY

SUNSTONE
PRESS

SANTA FE

Portions of Chapter 5 were taken from an interview of Alice Marriott
by Mary Lou Cook in 1987

Sunstone books may be purchased for educational, business, or sales
promotional use. For information please write:
Special Markets Department, Sunstone Press,
P.O. Box 2321, Santa Fe, New Mexico 87504-2321

Book design › Vicki Ahl
Body typeface › CG Omega ◇ Display typeface › Charlemagne Std
Printed on acid free paper

Library of Congress Cataloging-in-Publication Data

Marriott, Alice Lee, 1910-1992.
  Alice Marriott remembered / edited and with an introduction and annotations
by Charlotte Whaley.
     p. cm.
  ISBN 978-0-86534-697-0 (softcover : alk. paper)
  1. Marriott, Alice Lee, 1910-1992. 2. Women anthropologists–New Mexico–
Biography. 3. United States. Indian Arts and Crafts Board--History. 4. Martínez,
María Montoya. 5. Tewa women potters–New Mexico–San Ildefonso Pueblo.
6. Navajo Indians–New Mexico–Social life and customs. 7. Hopi Indians--New
Mexico–Social life and customs. I. Whaley, Charlotte, 1925- II. Title.
  GN21.M2577M37 2009
  301.092–dc22
  [B]
                                2009006114

WWW.SUNSTONEPRESS.COM
SUNSTONE PRESS / POST OFFICE BOX 2321 / SANTA FE, NM 87504-2321 /USA
(505) 988-4418 / ORDERS ONLY (800) 243-5644 / FAX (505) 988-1025

C O N T E N T S

Alice Marriott. Courtesy James Neill Northe, n.d.

INTRODUCTION

My late husband, Gould, and I recognized early in our post retirement careers as publishers of our own Still Point Press that a book about the famous American Southwest anthropologist/ethnographer Alice Marriott (1910–1992) would be an interesting and important one to have on our list. In addition to her most popular book, *Maria: The Potter of San Ildefonso* (1948), she authored or co-authored nineteen books and dozens of articles focusing on the diverse cultures of the Southwestern American Indian.

Alice was in very poor health and virtually blind in February 1987 when, at the suggestion of our mutual friend Margaret Lefranc Schoonover (artist and illustrator of many of Alice's books), we first approached her about writing her autobiography. Three weeks later Alice responded to my letter, saying there was no particular reason

for the delay—"just that typing is sometimes difficult for me."
And as for Margaret Schoonover's praise of her work, Alice said,
"Margaret is an amazing person. All her geese are swans; she
believes in them sincerely, and wants them to see each other
in her own glowing light." In addition to the letter, Alice sent
us an unpublished manuscript, "Spanish-American Folk Stories
of Some of New Mexico Saints," written in 1982. The stories
she had written down had been told to her by José de la Cruz
Romero (Alice's and Martha's talkative handyman, Maclovio
Salazar, in *The Valley Below*, 1949), but the dialect was so
heavy it was almost unreadable. When I called and mentioned
the difficulty we had in "translating" it, Alice became defensive:
"In New Mexico, at the time Cruz told me the stories, we all used
a Spanish shading in family conversations. Far from being a mark
of patronization or disdain, it was a mark of warm friendship and
trust. It *meant* something in the relationship between speaker
and listener. And in this case it gave an added conviction to
the stories. In New Mexico thirty-odd years ago, if there were
any segregation or patronization, it worked the other way. We
were called Anglos, with a down pitch to the 'o,' and we were
segregated."

We assured her that we would consider the Cruz
manuscript, possibly changing some of the heaviest sections of
dialect, such as "There's loots San Juans. So many eet's hard to
tahl wheech you talkin' 'bout." But we reminded her that we

were hoping for more about herself and her career; we wanted an *autobiography* of Alice Marriott.

She went back to work, but after a few futile attempts to produce a typewritten manuscript, she realized that she was too handicapped to continue. She called us from Oklahoma City, where she shared a home with her colleague Carol K. Rachlin, apologized, thanked us for our interest, and regretted that she was no longer able to write. We then asked her to consider taping her memoirs. While she had never done that, she agreed to give it a try. I mailed her a small tape recorder, a number of cassettes, and a long letter of encouragement in which I asked a few questions to help her get started, such as "What drew you to New Mexico? What were your first impressions of the Southwest as a whole and of Santa Fe in particular? When did you first meet José de la Cruz?"

Some months passed before the first tape arrived in the mail with a shaky hand-written letter from Alice describing her difficulty using a recorder—"I'm still eye-minded rather than ear-minded," she wrote. I transcribed the tape as best I could (her speech was slurred) and returned it for approval and editing. More months passed before we found another tape in the mailbox and another letter lamenting her struggle with dictation: "The tape recorder and I try to spend at least an hour a day making faces at each other. It's slow work and I don't at all like the battery-powered woman who lives in the machine. But give up? No!"

Alice had reservations about tape recorders when she first began her serious studies of Indian cultures in the Southwest. In 1952 she wrote: "tape recorders undoubtedly have their place in the ethnological world. But I imagine that both the ethnologist and the informant must go through a prolonged training process before being able to use a recorder to the best advantage. And since the material recorded by the machine must ultimately be transcribed anyway, I stick to the old notebook and pencil. The tape recorder alone will never be entirely satisfactory. It can catch words and nuances of intonation that the notebook cannot record fully, true enough. But it cannot catch the subtle shades of gesture, the lift of a brow or the turn of a wrist, that an observant eye can note and a quick hand jot down." Nevertheless, she realized that since her eyesight was virtually gone, taping her memoirs in 1987 was the only possible way to complete the assignment we had given her.

After Alice received my latest transcriptions she wrote: "I'm scared to look at the transcripts you sent. I know the work is bad, and I really don't want to find out HOW BAD. As of this moment I feel the whole business is a mistake, and if it weren't for you I'd build a fire in the fireplace, hot as the weather is." This was alarming news. She had actually burned the manuscript of her first book, *The Ten Grandmothers* (1945), started over, and produced a book that received glowing reviews and stayed in print for decades. "Please don't be discouraged," I quickly responded, "remember the old SMU Press adage: 'Don't get it right; get it written.' You are making a valuable contribution. Carol, keep her away from that fireplace!"

A week later Alice sent me another letter written in an unsteady hand, saying "I'm going over the transcripts and I wonder why in the world you bother with me—I'm not worth your generous misuse of time. It proves that I knew what I was talking about when I warned you that Margaret's geese are swans. It's been a tough summer—my eye getting worse and Carol's are developing cataracts; my poor old white poodle, Tessa, trying to find her way out of this world and into St. Francis's. I think that is the hardest of all, to watch a creature who has never known anything but loving and being loved enduring slow pain which she can't understand. Well I'll try to keep plugging, but don't expect much."

Meanwhile back in Dallas we were having our own crises. My sister Sheila was undergoing her tenth radiation treatment after fifty-one days in the hospital following surgery for lung cancer (she died a few weeks later), and Gould was showing alarming signs of dementia (which slowly progressed into full-blown Alzheimer's disease). I had another letter from a very discouraged Alice: ". . . end of tape. And about time, too. I don't think I've ever read anything quite so disgraceful and disgusting. And I certainly wouldn't have believed I could write anything so awful. I'll ask you to send all the existing transcripts back to me. They need to be edited with a pair of scissors, and I think I'd better do it myself, for penance, if for no other reason. Meantime, I'll try to work out a table of contents, or outline, or précis. I have never worked without one before, but all my kind friends have insisted that with a tape recorder it wasn't needed." She included her outline and first draft of "By Their Works You Shall Know Them," which traced the development of North American Indian arts and crafts.

Two weeks later Alice's letters had a more positive tone: "I've got started on the outline, and life looks rosier than it has in years. Let's face it, I'm a creature of habit. I was trying to stand without a floor. Now my feet are on the ground. In November she sent "Life on the Mesa," focusing on her experience with the Hopis. It was the best work she had submitted so far, even though the last ten pages were missing. Alice sent them later.

Her Christmas 1987 letter was upbeat and chatty: "I'm firmly resolved to find some worthy recipient and get rid of the tape recorder. Typing isn't much slower or more laborious, and makes better sense. I proceed by what Margaret calls 'stits and farts.' The question of what book I am writing is still moot. Carol's black poodle chases squirrels. In her last burst of energy, Mabel tried to climb the pecan tree to catch the latest intruder. She fell from a branch eight feet off the ground, and landed on her tail, to the squirrel's great amusement. But she broke her tail. She now wears her tail in a pressure bandage, and we hope a threatened amputation will not take place."

Hoping to speed things up, Gould and I decided to take a trip to Oklahoma City and meet Alice in person. This was after we had invited Alice and Carol to come to Dallas at our expense—we had made reservations for them on Southwest Airlines and a room at the Ramada Hotel for two days. I wrote to Alice, giving her the flight schedule and saying we would meet them at Love Field. "I'll be the one holding aloft a copy of one of your books—perhaps *These Are the People* would be most appropriate." Margaret Lefranc Schoonover was also planning to be in Dallas at that time, so I told Alice that I anticipated "a lively and interesting time for the five of us." Unfortunately, Alice came down with a bad cold the day before she was to leave and I had to cancel the reservations. Several weeks later we had a letter from Carol inviting us to come to visit them in Oklahoma City the first weekend in February 1988. She wrote: "Alice and I feel it would be more fruitful for you to come here, especially at this time of year. Alice gets tired easily and travel is difficult for her. There always has to be a rest up time after any trip. We both hope that you can come. In fact we are looking forward to it. Your visit will make the whole project a reality."

Carol's invitation was immediately followed by a letter from Alice: "I believe I have finally licked the tape recorder problem. I am writing on the typewriter; then reading to the machine, and sending the tapes to you to be used on your transcriber. I'm very happy about it. The writing goes slowly and is as good as any I've done in a long time. (For that 'slowly' read 'smoothly.')

"Carol says she sent you an invitation, and that she hopes you and your husband can and will accept it. Add mine to hers. It would be far easier to have you both here than to try to pull up stakes and go to Dallas, and I'm a lazy beast at best. I would like to meet you both, in this house. Anyway, here or there, I do want to go over what I'm doing with you, and get your suggestions for improvement, and then go on, following them as much as I can. I may as well admit that I have been scared to death about this whole business. I think it is better to postpone any conversation about books until my ego is once again its old spoiled objectionable self. If you haven't realized, and I don't talk much about it, I've taken a hell of a beating over the last ten years. You've helped a lot with the recovery, and I want to keep things as they are for a while longer.

"Anyway, as the Indian ladies used to say to Carol when she finally completely lost her hearing, 'I've just got to keep on agoin'.'"

On Friday, February 5, 1988, Gould and I flew off to Oklahoma City, rented a Ford Escort (whose shoulder belts, we discovered after many unsuccessful attempts to fasten them, tracked back on their own only after the ignition switch was turned on), and after many missed turns finally found the

Waterford Hotel. There waiting for us in the lobby were Alice and Carol, Alice with white hair and very dark glasses, a metal, four-pronged cane at her side, her face distorted by Bell's Palsy. Sitting next to her feeble friend was Carol—short, healthy, energetic, engaging, and quite deaf. She shouted when she had something to say during the long lunch at the hotel and later at their home, where we met the two poodles, Tessa and Mabel. Mabel still had her broken tail in a bandage. After admiring the house and dogs, Gould and I returned to the hotel to read the beginning of Alice's current manuscript and rest before joining them for a delicious pot-roast dinner carefully prepared by Carol. They both insisted that we have a late popover breakfast with them the next morning.

At breakfast, Gould suggested that Alice write about her most famous Indian subjects: Maria and Julián (stars of her highly acclaimed book *Maria: The Potter of San Ildefonso*). Alice demurred, saying she would have to think it over for several weeks. While Gould and Alice talked, I kept Carol busy answering and asking questions that I would write on slips of paper, a much easier way to communicate. I had brought my camera but Alice would not consent to being photographed. Time and old age had not been kind to her. Before we left to catch our flight back to Dallas, I promised to send her copies of our press's award-winning books and urged her to continue to record memories of her full and fascinating life.

Carol offered to guide us to the home of James Neill Northe, whom we thought dealt in antiquarian books (we were avid book collectors at that time), but she lost her way and signaled us to stop on a side street. She got out of her car, shouted at us to go to the other side of the freeway, shook hands, and took off very fast in her battered Subaru. After many wrong turns we finally found Northe's home. He was being interviewed by a young newspaperman when we arrived, an interview we discovered later had been going on for four hours. He was ninety-four years old in 1988 but looked and acted twenty years younger (we heard that he had had six wives). We learned that Northe did not sell books, only searched for those that were out of print. He urged us to return "when we can visit. A four-hour interview leaves me a bit out of the world." But he did have an excellent photograph of Alice in her prime, which he mailed to us a few days after we returned to Dallas. "Of the thousands of photographs I have taken," he wrote, "I feel this is one of the best: for the reason that it is a typical picture of Alice."

Gould and I then made our way to the airport and back to Dallas, but not before locking ourselves out of the Ford Escort, which we had parked in front of Northe's home. We called AAA, waited thirty minutes for the locksmith, who opened the car in ten seconds but only after he had broken into his own locked van to get the necessary tools. He had forgotten his own keys. I was glad to be home, but depressed with the all-too-obvious signs of the old-age crocodile moving in on all of us. Poor Gould's memory was worsening—he forgot to tip for service at the hotel, left his overcoat on the hall table when we checked out (the hotel clerk caught us before we drove off), and gave up in despair when he could not operate the car's headlights. It became necessary to recheck almost everything he did at that time, which was frustrating for both of us.

Alice's health was also failing. In March 1988, she wrote that she was "home and using a walker," healing from a broken hip, but was determined to return to her Maria & Julián manuscript. She had just learned about the work of a young Indian artist, Tony Jojola, who designed beautiful glass pottery. "Time was," she wrote, "when the idea of Maria pottery in glass would have curled my hair, but times change. I promptly fell in love with 'White Evergreen' [a stunning glass pot, reminiscent of Maria's style, with electroformed copper, 1987]. As soon as I could, I phoned the artist for permission to reproduce it [in the book she was writing for us]. 'Yes,' he said."

I had sent Alice copies of two slender books that we hoped would serve as models for "Remembering Maria" (our working title at the time): *My New Mexico Friends* by Lawrence Clark Powell, and *One Writer's Beginnings* by Eudora Welty.

The demands of Still Point Press and a husband who was showing more frightening signs of dementia interfered with my correspondence. Most of our discussions of Alice's pending manuscript took place over the telephone. In a letter to her on May 24, 1988, I summarized the contents of the work she had sent us. Her focus was on important friendships she had made during her long career as an ethnologist.

Among those who had appeared in the transcripts, in addition to Maria and Julián Martinez of San Ildefonso Pueblo, was René d'Harnoncourt (1901-1968), administrator of the Indian Arts and Crafts Board of the U.S. Department of Interior, with whom Alice had a strong personal and professional friendship. Another of her influential friends was Mary Cabot Wheelwright (1878–1958), founder with Navajo Indian Hastiin Klah of the Wheelwright Museum of the American Indian (now in Santa Fe), which contains world-renowned collections documenting Navajo art and culture. Writer Oliver La Farge (1901-1963) and Alice became good friends, since New-Mexico-based La Farge spent much of his adult life championing the rights of the American Indian. With Alice's memories of these distinguished people and others—Frederic H. (Eric) Douglas, Curator of Indian Art at the Denver Art Museum; artist Margaret Lefranc Schoonover, illustrator of six of Alice's books; fellow anthropologist Carol Rachlin, co-author with Alice of five books; Hopi painter and silversmith Fred Kabotie, and others—I was optimistic that given the information in Turner Kobler's short biobibliographical pamphlet, *Alice Marriott*, we could produce a book that would please us all.

I wanted to get started at our vacation home in Las Dos, twelve miles west of Santa Fe, and I urged Alice and Carol to join us the summer of 1988 for another face-to-face visit. That July, however, while trimming some shrubs around our Dallas home, I disturbed a family of wasps, one of which stung me on my right arm. To avoid more stings, I stepped away, fell backward over a full bag of yard trash, and broke both of my wrists. Three weeks after the accident I was able to use my gentle word-processing keyboard to hunt and peck the news to Alice.

"Lord help us," Alice wrote back, "what a series of catastrophes! Wasp stings are bad enough; one broken wrist is enough for anybody, but wasps and both wrists! That is a gilded rose, indeed! We've been having a time of our own. Not the [broken] hip. That is angelic. But all of a sudden I couldn't see, and I couldn't hear. Not seeing is old stuff by now, but the hearing is a different matter. Now I'm fitted with a cute little gadget in each ear, and the seeing is slightly improved. But if that weren't enough, you talked Carol into a computer. Not just a lone, lornly word processor, but a printer and all the rest of the works. So we moved all the office furniture, and a hellish amount of books, and she is reestablished. Then my typewriter gave out. The "H" and "h" became snaggle-toothed. I tried substituting. The method I liked best was to use "?" instead of upper or lower case letter sticks. I inherited Carol's typewriter—this one—because I am not about to struggle with another new set of habit patterns just now.

"And I'm scared of the thing anyway. I'm not used to machinery that can think faster than I can.

"Now I'm torn about you. If I go back to work, on what may turn out to be an even natural pace, you may work harder than you should. But if I don't go back to work, you'll fuss about having nothing to do. Well, I can sit in the middle of a little dilemma as well as the next woman!

"If nothing else happens, and our friends the Wyants have room for us, we'll get a few days in Santa Fe in September. Remarking that the weather will be a nice change is unnecessary to anyone in Dallas. But it will be. Please, please, please for everybody's sake, take care of yourself and stay away from brush fires."

By September 1988 my wrists had healed and we arranged to see Alice and Carol for lunch at our home in Santa Fe. Margaret Lefranc Schoonover was also in residence at that time. After a long and amiable meal, we adjourned to the living room, where I had hoped I could have some time with Alice to go over the work she had been sending me off and on over the past two years. Carol, however, had other plans for Alice—a shopping trip around the Santa Fe plaza. Because Carol was totally deaf at that time she could not understand why she and Alice were lingering at the house when they should have been heading back to town. For about thirty minutes Gould, Alice, and

I tried to discuss the business of the book we hoped to publish, but Carol's loud protests and impatient pacing around the room won out. We bid them goodbye, and later wondered if this star-crossed project was worth the effort.

Two weeks later, Alice wrote to thank us for the lunch and express her hope that "before too long we can foregather at one end of the commuter flight for some serious talking and thinking. Santa Fe just wasn't the place—too many people, each with a separate set of demands. That includes Carol and Margaret. Each of them is used to my undivided attention, and when she doesn't get it there are wigs on the green. And neither of them likes to be left out of anything. Actually, they both think I am a lot stronger and more supple than I am. I don't apologize for what must have seemed rudeness on my part, and I can't apologize for anyone else.

"We are beginning to get shook out and pulled together. I can even think about working again. The combination of a Santa Feish flu bug and a full-length fall on the tiled bathroom floor has interfered with my mental processes. I'm beginning to figure out where to go from here, and the best way to travel to get there. As the last of the dinosaurs, I feel an obligation to get the show on the road."

Alice went on to reminisce about the rich friendships she had made during the seven years (1935–1942) before World War II. "So many people, and such unexpected strengths!"

While two writers [perhaps she meant Russell Lynes and Robert Fay Schrader] had written about René d'Harnoncourt in an official capacity as a United States government servant with the Department of the Interior, Alice maintained that they "managed to miss personalities and the inter-operation," overlooking such interesting details as "the tragedy of having the insigne of the Knights of Malta ripped off his sleeve, so he would look like any other man in evening dress."

As she went back over those seven years, Alice felt as if she had lived her whole life then. "Certainly the most interesting part of it. I sat and looked up the face of Puye Cliff this time [September 1988] and could still see Lenore Sloan in her full black skirt, climbing the pole ladders even when the wind turned the skirt inside out over her head, while Eric Douglas rocked with laughter at the top and tried to steady the poles for her. My first cliff dwelling, and I rather suspect, my last, now that it's getting harder and harder to see anything. I'd better get on with the job while I can still do it.

"Or I can see Eric, who was driving Lenore in his car while I pounded behind with Mabel Morrow in mine, when we went through Cordova and a goat tethered on a house top baaed at us. My first glimpse of Cordova, but far from my last, although it took World War II to get me back there. Santa Fe and its environs will always be haunted by the ghosts of those I loved, and it isn't always easy to write about them. I know everyone has an attic full of unexpected and unexplained memories—that's what's holding me back."

That was the last letter I received from Alice, with its intriguing reference to "an attic full of unexpected and unexplained memories." And my last letter to her mentioned the arrival of Still Point Press's *Battle Stations* by Tom Lea, which I and a friend were busy distributing. I urged Alice to continue working on her delightful reminiscences of old friends and experiences, whether explained or not.

Three years and three months later, on March 18, 1992, Alice Marriott died. For two years prior to her death—1989 to 1991—most of our communication took place over the telephone. Despite her failing eyesight and other physical infirmities, she bravely tried off and on to write more of her memoirs, but she never completed them. During those three years I was writing a biography of the pioneering woman who homesteaded the land where we built our vacation home in 1982—*Nina Otero Warren of Santa Fe* (University of New Mexico Press, 1994; Sunstone Press, 2007), and dealing with the publication of the last Still Point Press book, *Stanley Marcus: A Life with Books* by David Farmer, 1992. Alzheimer's disease had so debilitated Gould that he could not fold in half promotional brochures of the Marcus book for mailing. Five years later, in 1997, I closed Still Point Press.

I learned of Alice's death from Margaret Lefranc Schoonover, who called with the sad news, and I immediately wrote to Carol Rachlin to offer condolences: "Gould and I are thinking of you with affection and sympathy, knowing what a great void her death has left in your life. I want to assure you, and Alice if she is listening from the astral plane, that we do want to pursue the publication of that book we talked about in 1989.

"I read somewhere that we can all learn much from illness and death—both restore the sense of value and proportion that we lose when we take life for granted. Alice certainly understood that. What a full and productive, and valuable, life she had. We truly feel thankful that we had the chance to know her and to work with her—and with you. Love and courage through these coming difficult weeks."

Margaret also wrote Carol, suggesting that a foundation in Alice's name be established as a permanent memorial to her, "perhaps in conjunction with the University of Central Oklahoma, to financially aid Indian students. Alice was one of the few whose energies in life made a difference—a difference in the shaping of the world's view about Indians of the United States. Let us honor her for that."

Gould and I never heard from Carol. In researching this book, I went to the Internet and found her address (still on 56th Street in Oklahoma City) and telephone number. On January 9, 2008, I called and talked with Myra, Carol's caregiver, who wrote down my queries to the deaf eighty-eight-year-old woman and showed them to her. I learned that Alice's papers were in the Western Library of the University of Oklahoma, Norman.

The New York Times ran an obituary of Alice Lee Marriott three days after her death. According to Margaret Lefranc Schoonover, the Times reported, Alice died of heart failure. "Miss Marriott," the article continued, "was not the first to study Americans Indians, but she promoted an appreciation of their culture by a wide audience and helped break the stereotypes of Indians as uncivilized savages. 'Indians are not beautiful, quaint and exotic creatures, like museum pieces,' she said in an interview in 1963. 'They have a very rich and very complex culture of deep metaphysical and philosophical meaning'."

The only published detailed biographical information about Alice Marriott, other than the glimpses she gave us in her books Greener Fields and The Valley Below, was written by Turner S. Kobler in 1969 as part of the Southwest Writers Series, published by Steck-Vaughn Company, in Austin, Texas. There we find that Alice was born in Wilmette, Illinois, January 8, 1910, then moved with her family to Oklahoma City at the age of seven. Her father, Richard Goulding Marriott, was employed as treasurer of an insurance company; her mother, Sydney Kenner Cunningham Marriott, "daughter of a very old Southern family," was a CPA. Her maternal grandmother, an avid reader, lived with the family and it was from her that Alice inherited her "capacious memory" and her strong motivation to read (she began at age two) and learn.

Young Alice Marriott. Courtesy University of Oklahoma, Norman, Oklahoma, n.d., Photo #596

Early on Alice showed an interest in her British-born grandfather's avocation as an amateur Egyptologist, although the five-year-old was more taken with the Field Museum of Natural History's exhibit of Indian totem poles and of the beautiful stone points she found around her family's home. Her gifts as a writer became evident when she won a prize for a short story she entered in a Central High School literary contest. She excelled in college as well, graduating *magna cum laude,* Phi Beta Kappa, with a B. A. degree in English from Oklahoma City University in 1932. After a two-year hiatus, during which she worked as a cataloger at the public library in Maskogee, Oklahoma, she followed her dream to discover more about the American Indian. In 1935 she took another bachelor's degree, this one in anthropology from the University of Oklahoma (at that time no advanced degrees were awarded in anthropology). In the process she discovered that she had extraordinary gifts for interviewing—her tact and her ability to make others comfortable, easily eliciting from her informants detailed answers to her probing questions. She also could write about serious ethnographic matters without the usual scientific jargon. Added to this were her strong work ethic (she published twenty books and dozens of articles and book reviews) and her ability to form trusting, lasting relationships with her Indian friends and other distinguished leaders in her field.

One of the first indications of the strong rapport she had

with Indians came in 1936, after two summers of field work with the Kiowas. The elders of the tribe, encouraged by Spear Woman (Alice's principal informant), decided to adopt this twenty-six-year-old Anglo woman and call her "Hummingbird Girl." "Why Hummingbird Girl?" Alice asked. Because, Spear Woman said, "you've got red hair like a hummingbird's top knot. . . .You never keep still a minute. If you aren't writing, you're chewing on your pencil or wiggling around or scratching your head—your hands go, go like a hummingbird's wings, all the time." Her enormous energy and productivity were interpreted differently by the Cheyennes, who called her "Spirit Woman" (*Mah-hee-yuna*).

Spirited, energetic, and dedicated to the task at hand, Alice could be profound and contemplative, calm and detached, lively and entertaining (though always ethnologically factual) when writing about cultures not her own. And although she was nearing the end of her life when the pieces that comprise this book were recorded or written, that same spirit prevails. Once more we are given insight into the people and events that Alice Marriott remembered.

—Charlotte Whaley
Dallas and Las Dos

1

A CAREER IS LAUNCHED

ALL OF US are what our friends have made us. Friends may be members of one's immediate family, lovers or husbands or wives; they may be anything you like in other capacities. But friends they remain, and their influence on you is an enduring and sometimes endearing one.

I think, from the top of my head, of René d'Harnoncourt, who was for seven years the general manager of the Indian Arts and Crafts Board. René had been born in Austria and trained there as an engineer, before the Austrian Empire disintegrated at the end of World War I. René did what many young men of the nobility did—he took himself over to the West. He went to

Mexico, and in Mexico City he met and began to work with Fred Davis, who was a North American citizen of the United States and a man deeply and profoundly concerned with Mexican Indian folklore, folklife, folkways, and all that those terms imply. René was a quick learner. He put what he learned from Mr. Davis to work with what he had learned at the University of Vienna, and came up with a combination of skills that was peculiarly his own.

One thing I remember being told about René was his constructing a window display for a drugstore chain, in which a man was shown seated in a rocking chair, tilting backward and forward mechanically, and with a most unhappy and woeful look on his face. At regular intervals he clapped his hand to his middle and arose, moved by the same mechanical devices that powered the chair, into the wings of the display windows, and returned immediately thereafter with a happy smile on his face and a bottle of laxative clutched in his hand. That was one of the first animated window displays anybody ever saw anywhere, and it was a tremendous success.

During the years that René worked with Mr. Davis, he became acquainted with many citizens of the United States. (I wish I could use the word *Americans*, but I don't like to in this context. Actually, Mexicans are Americans and very proud of it. So I'll try to avoid the expression by circumlocution.) Among the people whom René met in Mexico City were Dwight and

Elizabeth Morrow and members of their family, and the John Collier circle of movers and shakers and reformers which was originally organized by Mabel Dodge Luhan and which spread and spread all over the do-good society of the United States. These introductions in turn led to others, as they generally do, and René at last became a friend of very many of the people who were most influential and most positive in work for the American Indians.

When John Collier was appointed Commissioner of Indian Affairs under Harold Ickes in the first F. D. Roosevelt and Eleanor Roosevelt administration [1933–1936], he looked around for sources of income for a woefully poverty-oppressed people. At that time, the average family income of a Choctaw group in Oklahoma—southeastern Oklahoma—was $49.50 per annum. This was rock bottom, I'll admit, and even the Navajos, who were held up as shining examples of poverty in other rural areas, had a family income of $200 per annum. Of course, we must say that the Navajos had bigger families than the Choctaws. The Choctaws have paid a heavy toll in life expectancy to hook worm, malaria, tuberculosis, and venereal disease. The Navajos, more or less isolated in the nice clean desert, had not had this great chance to make of themselves an almost ruined people.

Indian arts and crafts at that time fell into two classifications: there were the objects that could be bought at the railroad stations as the Santa Fe train moved west, and there were those which were made by Indians for Indians, traded, exchanged, or almost used as bartered currency among themselves. Neither situation was satisfactory to Mr. Collier or to Mr. and Mrs. Ickes, the first Mrs. Ickes [Anna Wilmarth Thompson Ickes]. She had become enamored of the Navajo, as many people do, and stirred the world with her accounts of the beauty of the desert, the beauty of its people, the magnificent crafts work in textiles and metal, and the other things that the Navajos produced as they became quite independent of other nations. It was evident that arts and crafts would be one way out of the maze of poverty in which not only Choctaws and Navajos, but most Indians in the United States found themselves at that time. With the blessing of Mrs. Roosevelt, the Indian Arts and Crafts Board was organized. At least, it was organized on paper; it was never really organized.

A question that was often asked during the decade of the 1930s was why have an Indian Arts and Crafts Board anyway? Nowhere in human history have we found such a record of pampering of victims of captivity by the victors. I can think of nowhere else that a government agency has been created for the sole care and feeding of what were supposed to be the mercilessly and hopelessly lost of any society.

After all, the Indians of the United States had a bureau of their own under the shelter of the Department of the Interior. Could not that bureau be split up to accommodate the arts and crafts among all its other Indian services? Why must the Department of the Interior have a Department of Indian Forestry in addition to its Department of National Parks, the Division of National Forests, the Division of Plant Ecology, the Division of Fisheries, and innumerable other organizations designed solely to perpetuate and emphasize the skills and manufactures of a captive people?

The answer is not simple. It can be put in the form of a bureau, organization, or department that took care of all the odds and ends of the other departments, or did not conform to a national educational program, did not even teach or perpetuate skills that would have otherwise been lost. The Indian Arts and Crafts Board in its inception was engaged in the preservation of crafts and arts, in teaching skills to the younger people, and in creating a whole school of easel art that still endures. True, there were times when easel artists deserted their flat beds and took to wall painting; murals by Indian painters were extremely fashionable in the late 1930s. And there again, a prehistoric cultural trait was perpetuated, because the walls of kivas and of the partitions of the long houses of the Arctic Circle had this in common—that they were painted on walls.

Looking around for someone to help him develop this Indian arts and crafts idea, Mr. Collier addressed a letter to Mr. Davis. Davis, with a sweet smile on his face (I am told), returned the compliment by suggesting that since he was extremely busy with his own business in Mexico City, René d'Harnoncourt should take on the job of general manager of the Indian Arts and Crafts Board. In the meantime, a friend of Mrs. Ickes from Cincinnati, Ohio—Mr. Lewis C. West—had been appointed temporarily as general manager. René began work as Mr. West's assistant.

Mr. West survived approximately three months of the Indian Arts and Crafts Board, the country in which Indians lived, the Indians themselves, and weather and climatic conditions unlike those native to Ohio. I know this because I was the first field representative appointed to the Indian Arts and Crafts Board by anyone, and I was kind of dragged out of the bottom of the barrel because somebody had to represent the Indians of Oklahoma, Kansas, and Texas—always referred to in that order. There were not that many people with any kind of training to go around.

The first year of the Board's existence was completed by a sequence of trials and errors participated in by everyone concerned. Mr. West managed to hurt the feelings—and believe me, the feelings were easily hurt—of practically all of the leading Indians in the United States at that time who were literate and literary and resigned. According to President Roosevelt, nobody could do a thing with Lewis West. He was Eleanor's boy and Eleanor's boy he remained. How much of this information is apocryphal and how much is actual I am in no position to say, because I was not there to hear it. I was out tootling around over the map of Oklahoma, looking up Indians I knew, dropping in on Indians I did not know, and searching frantically through hock shops for surviving samples of old-time Indian arts and crafts.

Now there is one very, very difficult thing to make clear. The arts and crafts that were produced for the Indian market for Indian use were beyond reproach. They were extremely beautiful. They were very, very complex in their construction, and they were not for sale. They went through hands successively, through generations successively, for that matter. But they never became a marketable commodity simply because too much time was required to produce them to make them economically feasible.

So we had in Oklahoma a situation which was immensely complex right to its roots. Almost all the tribes resided in Oklahoma at that time, and the government listed fifty-seven varieties of Indians in its annual reports. All had been removed to the area from other parts of the United States. We had Modocs from Oregon—survivors of the only war the United States ever lost to the Indians—living cheek by jowl with Senecas from New York, and all of them on friendly gossipy terms with Ottawas, Chippewas, and Cherokees, all packed into a little eight-mile-wide corner of a fairly large state.

The west side of Oklahoma was occupied by Indians that could be called *native*. Kiowa, Comanche, and Cheyenne, and the Arapaho, the Wichita, and some of the other Cadoan groups had been there from the beginning of written history. But they had come of their own free will into what was originally a lush, satisfactory and at the same time rather desolate section of the high plains.

So the beginning of the Indian Arts and Crafts Board in Oklahoma, as I saw it, consisted of finding people who knew something about Indian arts and crafts. René visited Oklahoma, he interviewed me, he decided, as he said, that I was a charming young lady but not diplomatic in manner, and that I must acquire "deeploemasee" immediately and forthwith if I were to deal, not with the Indians (they were easy) but with the various branches of the United States government field staff with which I would come in contact. This was a more difficult matter, because many of the administrators, like the Indians themselves, had been imported to Oklahoma from other parts of the country. They were fine righteous, painfully honest people in bulk, but they were also narrow minded, provincial, and inclined to foster segregation of Indians, Negroes, Jews, and foreigners generally from their scheme of social organization.

The terms "discrimination" and "ethnocentricity" had not then been coined. Several of the people of the United States Bureau of Indian Affairs with whom I came in contact in those years stand out in my memory, and always will. With some of them I worked diligently and hard, some of them had great sympathy, even empathy, for Indians; some of them were

Indians themselves, but Indians who had been educated in the Northeast. There is really nothing more confusing than to look at a tall upright Indian man with an unmistakable Cherokee name, such as Rainwater, and learn that he possesses a degree from the Harvard School of Law. Or that the doctor he is seeing on administrative business every day is enrolled as a member of the Ottowa tribe.

These contradictions had been so much a part of my life before I encountered the Indian Arts and Crafts Board that they had ceased to be contradictions. They just were the state of affairs. I was used to them, I could live with them, I could work with them, I had a good time with them. But none of these highly educated and very dictatorial gentlemen had the faintest idea of what I meant when I said "arts and crafts."

It was inevitable, then, that my work should fall with Indian women. And Indian women are a law unto themselves. At that time little had been written about them, or even reported about them, principally because the anthropologists who had come into the field to study American Indians were men, and they conceived a man-centered situation, enlarged upon it, developed it, made it as complex as it could be made, and forgot that a little over fifty percent of the population of any given Indian tribe was totally out of their scheme of things.

An exception is my corroborator Carol Rachlin, who for thirty years has studied the textiles of Indians of the eastern woodlands. When Carol first began her study of woodland weaving there was a small number of women around who knew the skills as taught to them by their mothers and grandmothers. Today there is only one person in the whole United States who is familiar technically and creatively with that particular type of weaving developed in the eastern woodlands. And that person in a non-Indian—Carol Rachlin, a graduate of Columbia University, among other places, and a skilled craftswoman in her own right.

Probably the skill would have perished completely with the final generation to be of the eastern tribes in the 1930s if Carol had not wound her way from the Atlantic coast to the Mississippi Valley and discovered a number of techniques that were unknown elsewhere. Nowhere is this type of weaving to be confused with the upright or flat handloom adapted by the Navajos and other western tribes from weaving cultures of Europe. Therefore, Carol not only perpetuated a craft—a suspended warp technique—that would otherwise have been lost, she put herself in a position to teach it to anybody else who wanted to learn it.

If the Indian Arts and Crafts Board were to survive at all, it had to be in terms of functionalism. And so we scrambled wildly, searching for things that could be functional, or that were functional, or could be consigned to the locus of art in its pure sense: as absolutely useless.

Indian metal art originally was a hammered style of working, using not only hammers but anvils. The silver or copper ore could be beaten thin on the anvil with a hammer, and then could be embossed, carved, and scratched on—anything to make it decorative. And Indian metalwork, while it was limited and confined to only some geographical parts of the United States, where reasonably pure ores could be removed from the ground, was a precious thing. It became a mark of distinction, of valor, and of many other recognizable cultural traits. But it was not usable in the sense that tools are usable. A copper headdress in the form of an embossed sheet, decorated with a persona of an eagle, could not be called useful, however ornamental it might be. And that was equally true with other metals.

It was not until the 1860s, when the Navajos were sent on a long walk from the Four Corners country to southeastern New Mexico, to the swamps of the Bosque Redondo that metalwork among Indians came to have a practical saleable value. Indian draftsmen, deprived of their usual materials in which to work, soon perceived that silver coins were valuable to the troopers who guarded them. Coins could be hammered like ores, could be scratched on, could be ornamented in any one of a number of different ways and designs. And a whole school of southwestern silver working came eventually into being.

Another spurt of metalworking came with the cross-country railroads and the telegraph wires that paralleled them.

The telegraph wire was ideal for certain types of metalwork. It was soft, it was malleable, and it could be bent, twisted, and curved into all sorts of pieces. The same was true of brass artillery shells, which could be removed from the original casings and used to create bracelets, necklaces, and other adornments.

Turquoise had been known to Indians in the southwest for centuries as a beautiful and ornamental stone. Lignite, which is often called American Jet and is actually a form of coal, could be used to accent silver and turquoise, and shells had always been known and used in one form or another among Indian groups. So by the mid-1870s, when the Navajos walked the Long Road back from the Bosque Redondo to the Four Corners, they had acquired a characteristic style of their own in metalwork. They had seen the buttons worn on uniforms, they could see the jewelry worn by white women, and they had practiced and practiced until they had pounded out sheets of circles of silver from coins.

It cannot be said that an Indian painter or artist of any description is creative in the sense that European artists are, or have been. For example, the Barbizon School of Painting, impressionistic in style, is inconceivable in any Indian culture. It is something that is particularly and peculiarly non-Indian, or, as we say, Anglo cum Franco.

"Real" art, it would seem, had its place in the world and would continue to hold it. But was that place sufficient, and could a man or a woman make a living from it? So a secondary trend was to develop saleable crafts of Indian manufacture.

Adaptation was tried. Evening dresses were decorated with ribbon appliqué in various styles. All kinds of hats became baskets, and baskets became hats became handbags became carryalls—all starting with storage containers. Pottery had never completely left the Southwest, but it was totally unusable in the European sense of the word, because it was soft-fired and the introduction of a drop of water to a piece of southwestern pottery without previously varnishing the pot is disastrous. The water falls out and the sides fall in and there you sit with the aboriginal piece of mud before you.

I talk about pottery because I like pottery. I've learned to make it, but I can't for the life of me see why I should make, or should encourage other people to make pottery that is totally nonfunctional. Were there a use for it, were there a place in the surrounding world where this pottery could be used for anything else but decoration we would not be faced with this problem. We would just go ahead and pot.

And so it was with many skills. They had a place in their world. Their potential in the other world, the outside world, was, we thought—we hoped—enormous. But to find that place always required adaptation, such as putting a coat of spar varnish on the interior of the pot, or the use of hemp and string for warps in woven baskets, or painting in tempera, which comes nearer to being an earth color on paper, although it has nothing to do with the Indians.

But things are changing, more so in the Indian cultures in the United States than anywhere else I can name. Indians will always be Indians, whether they are hyphenated [i.e.: American-Indian] or not, but as I discovered soon after I began my study of Indian cultures, their arts and crafts had certain distinctive characteristics—humor, warmth, and, at that time, a total lack of imagination.

But it is now possible to identify artists personally, rather than tribally. For a long time, identification had been in terms of "Northern Plains," "Eastern Woodland," "Village Southwest," "probably Navajo," and so on. Then it became "Sioux," "Cheyenne," "Arapaho," "Seminole," etc.—all recognizable as tribal styles, at least. Now it can be "Archie Black Owl," "Acee Blue Eagle," "Robert Chee," "Theodore Suaso," with a tribal identification attached if it is known.

Then there is the question of cultural identification, as exemplified by Bill Flores, a painter and medical illustrator for the AAA. Bill's father was a Papago from southeastern Arizona; his mother a Cherokee from northeastern Oklahoma. The result of this fantastic combination is striking and final. Tribal barriers were shattered thanks to the BIA's [Bureau of Indian Affairs] educational policy, and a new division of Indian cultures—Papago-Cherokee—came into existence.

So the Arts and Crafts Board blazed its mark on the tree trunks of a forest of confusions, after all. The one remaining confusion is as when Acee Blue Eagle, Pawnee-Creek (and that's a weird combination!) taught Archie Black Owl, then in his teens and a Cheyenne, how to paint in what is becoming known as "Kiowa style." And the next notable art teacher was Dick West, who taught all his students to paint in his own Cheyenne style, which he had learned as a boy from Steve Mopope, Kiowa. So you can take the Indian out of the boy, but the tribal influence remains in one form or another.

And now we have women painters, who are hyphenated in style and further hyphenated by marriage. Oh, what a tangled web the Bureau has woven!

2

ADVENTURES WITH FRIENDS IN THE FIELD

I HAVE BEEN ASKED what drew me to New Mexico. I had never been in New Mexico, except to go through on a train, previous to 1936 when I began work for the Indian Arts and Crafts Board. And I was frankly somewhat annoyed and very jealous of all the people who came from the Southwest into Oklahoma, looked at Indians who were making distinguished records in such professions as law and medicine and teaching, and informed me point blank and forthwith that I didn't know anything about Indians because I had never seen an Indian. I'd never seen a Navajo, God help us, and I'd never seen a Pueblo. So, that was that. They said I didn't know anything about Indians. No, I was not particularly drawn to New Mexico—I wanted to stay away from it. I was, as I say, jealous and frankly awfully bored with repetition from the higher-ups and the mighty-mighties who had been to New Mexico to take their vacations and thought it was just lovely.

I set about in the beginning to put the Indians living outside the Southwest on the map, as much as I could. I was lucky. I was assigned Oklahoma first. It was my home state; I belonged there anyhow. There is a certain fact about Oklahoma that I think few people have absorbed. That is that there are fifty-seven recognized Indian tribes—federally recognized that is—in the state. Fifty-seven varieties of Indians from all parts of the continent except Alaska. So anyone who works in Oklahoma for a considerable period of time is exposed to a great deal of Indian culture, and to a wide assortment of cultural behavior.

I went on from Oklahoma, first to Kansas, and from there on to Texas, and to what was left in Arkansas (very little), and then to the deep South—Mississippi, Alabama, Georgia, the Carolinas—and to the peninsula of Florida. From there I hopped, skipped, and jumped up to the Great Lakes area and the Indians of the eastern woodlands.

My first direct encounter with the capitalized Southwest was in 1938, and at that time I was assigned to teach anthropology in the Indian school at Riverside, California, the Sherman Institute, where the Bureau of Indian Affairs was holding a summer seminar for school teachers employed by the Bureau.

With my friend Lenore Sloan I set out to drive cross country to California, and that necessitated crossing New Mexico and Arizona. Our first real encounter with <u>real</u> Indians (in the locally accepted term) came on the Fourth of July in Flagstaff, Arizona, where we attended the Indian craftsmen's show at the Museum of Northern Arizona. To be quite frank, it seemed to me a pretty bad, lousy, set of craftsmen's shows. The Navajos had rugs and blankets. The Hopis had rugs and blankets. The Paiutes had fur rugs and blankets. (Incidentally, they didn't get all the lice out of the rugs and blankets.) And there was some pottery, and some pottery, and some pottery from many pueblos. And a few dances which were not really as spectacular as those that I was accustomed to seeing in Oklahoma.

But the weather was good; the mountains were lovely. We met Eric Douglas for the first time, and that was the beginning of a long and beautiful friendship between him and me, which has lasted past his death in 1956 to this day. I still think that Eric Douglas was one of the great men who lived and breathed and worked and talked—and talked and <u>talked</u>—in the Indian field.

Flagstaff, then as now, was the most exciting place in Arizona on the Fourth of July. There were not only displays of crafts, there were displays of people, people who ranged from full-skirted, dramatically striding Navajo women to short-skirted clumsy *turistas*, who figured, I suppose, that wide-brimmed hats were a sufficient substitute for an adequate supply of undergarments. These came and went, staggering against each other in the crowds, sneezing vociferously into bandanas or pieces of Kleenex, talking. One heard the *turistas* as well as saw them. One hardly heard or was conscious of the voices of the Navajo women—slow spoken quiet, controlled, but full of mirth as they viewed the costumes around them.

Deer Dancers, Buffalo Dancers, and Wild Turkey Woman at San Ildefonso Pueblo. Courtesy University of Oklahoma, Norman, Oklahoma, n.d., Photo #489

In the afternoon there was always a rodéo. It was the rodéo in those days before the Spanish influence had reversed itself, and ródeo had become the accepted pronunciation. This was the first ródeo I had seen and it was enormously exciting. I have never seen one since, and I've seen many, that had quite the drama and the flair and the stimulus of that first one in Flagstaff on the Fourth of July.

Eric, Lenore, and I sat perched in a row on wooden bleachers. We were sure they would collapse under us, but we didn't really care. They were wood. They might be full of splinters, but at least they weren't full of heavy flesh-piercing steel girders that could penetrate a human body in the breath of an instant and destroy everything and everybody around. There is something very soothing, very reassuring, about nailed-up-by-hand-the-night-before kind of wooden bleacher that I will never outgrow.

The men rode, the women did not ride. In fact, for a woman to have ridden in a ródeo at that time, even as a barrel-racer, was tabu. It was only at the end of the afternoon when all of the bulls had been buldogged, all of the cows had been milked into coke bottles, all of the excitement was enveloped in a cloud of dust, that the women had their moment of glory. Suddenly, the gate at the north side of the arena was flung open and through it galloped teams of horses drawing wagons, as nearly as possible abreast, each team driven by a Navajo woman, who stood on the footboard with a lash in one hand and the reins in the other, and lashed and drove the teams forward. Only two horses were allowed to a team. There was no stopping if one of them fell. The spectators simply rushed forward, dragged the wagon, woman, and horse, all kicking and screaming (except the wagon) to the sidelines, and the race went on, five times around the open arena. It has never ceased to give me the feeling that I have gone back in time to the days of Lew Wallace's *Ben-Hur*, and am watching a gladiator race in the Roman Coliseum (although I've never seen the Roman Coliseum), and I'm sure it was never as dusty as the arena in Flagstaff.

At night the fires were lighted. Each family stayed to itself. Sparks from piñon branches and the perfume of the smoke filled the air for a few brief hours. The grounds quieted and the sun sank. It was restful, peaceful, quiet, all together delightful at Flagstaff on the Fourth of July in those long-ago times.

I'm afraid I'm awfully sentimental about some things, and this is one of them, although I try not to be unnecessarily so. On the morning of the fifth of July, Lenore and I abandoned the Flagstaff ceremonial, as it was called. It wasn't ceremonial, except that it followed a somewhat allegorical pattern. We packed our belongings into the car and headed westward again across northern Arizona. We skirted the Grand Canyon and came down at Winslow on old Highway 66, which is still the route to follow, although the numbers of the highway have been changed. It is still the road to California.

That night we made it to the Nevada line, and there we stopped for the night. We had been warned not to go across the desert in the daylight if we could avoid it, so instead of going directly across the Mojave, we turned north to the Colorado River where it flowed over the Hoover Dam and created a spectacle of its own. Then we turned south again, out of Arizona, back into Arizona, and we stopped for dinner and to draw a deep breath about twenty-five miles out of Las Vegas on the main highway across the Mojave Desert.

About 11:00 P.M. the night was dark, and we decided it was time to venture forth and tackle the miles of Mojave desert that lay before us. We decided, but the car did not. The car was becoming very tired indeed. It didn't like the hot weather, it didn't like the blazing sunlight, and above all it disliked altitudes. I drove that beautiful bright green Lafayette sedan for a long time, but I never succeeded in winning the argument between the motor and me about going up a hill. Going down was all right, as long as the brakes held. But up, *no*. The car refused to go upward many times and often. This particular night it refused, fortunately, in front of a filling station, and there we found the one and only bright spot in what was rapidly becoming a very dismal night.

The man who owned the filling station was a retired locomotive engineer. He assured us that he knew all there was to know about any kind of engine, including those in automobiles, and he proceeded to go to work to put ours to rights. His wife hospitably offered us a cot apiece in a room behind the filling station, and there we subsided, worn and dusty and dirty and weary. And there we stayed.

That place was not conducive to restful sleep. In the first place, even before we got into the bedroom we saw something scuttering across the floor, as if a wider carpet was roaming before our eyes. When we directed a flashlight toward its margins we discovered insects. They were running, their tails were up and curled over their backs. There was a shivering movement within the room and its air seemed to throb.

"Scorpions," exclaimed Lenore, and turned and ran through the door in the opposite direction. I followed her, waving the flashlight, and hoping against hope that they were not scorpions but something else. We stopped in the weak light of the electric floods outside the filling station, and the people who ran the place came out. They looked at our white faces and our trembling hands in some surprise. "What happened?" they asked in chorus.

"I don't know," I stammered, "I don't know. They looked like scorpions. The tails were up over their backs and there were thousands, millions, of them."

"Well, well," said the man who was going to repair the car, "I guess them was vinegaroons."

We learned that a "vinegaroon" is a whip scorpion that emits a vinegary odor when disturbed so we refused point blank to return to the vinegaroon-infested sleeping place and spent the night sitting up in stiff, straight-backed chairs in the office of the filling station. Just as dawn was breaking in the east, the former locomotive engineer approached us and announced, "She's ready girls. I reckon you can take 'er on down the road."

"How far can I take her?" I asked.

"Well, I wouldn't want to say exactly, but I do say that you should take her no farther than Barstow. They rent rooms at a tourist court there on a daily basis. You can get an all-day sleeping place, and you better have it. You look tuckered out—both of you—and some rest would do you good. Besides that, you don't want to go beyond Barstow by daylight. It's too rough a road."

So we chugged and chugged and chugged our way to Barstow, California, where we found a tourist court that advertised "Rooms by the Day, Not Night." We took a room, regardless of the fact that it had only a double bed and we were used to sleeping singly, and brought in what luggage we thought we needed for the night—or, rather, the day. We went to sleep, really dejectedly, but to sleep, and we slept until the tourist court office rang the bell of the telephone and announced "All out! It's dark."

Dark it might be, but we could not go on without some

nourishment. There was an all-night café down the road, and there we found bacon, eggs, coffee, toast, all the things that we were accustomed to eating for breakfast. It seemed to us exorbitantly overpriced, but as Lenore said at the time, if you're hungry, you eat, and if you have money to pay for it, you pay for it. And we paid for it, not only in money, but as it later turned out, in indigestion.

I don't remember much about that desert crossing now. I know that it was all driven in the dark. The car lights sent a pool of illumination ahead, and I know too that somewhere, somehow, just outside of town, our fifth tire blew. We couldn't repair it ourselves. Neither of us knew how, and we sat marooned by the roadside for about half an hour. Then I gathered my courage in both hands, and turned to Lenore. "You stay here and watch the car," I said. "I'm going into town."

"Where is town?"

"I don't know, but I rather guess it's down the road apiece. That's what they say around here." And I started out.

Actually, I thought we were on the outskirts of the town. I tried to march as bravely as any soldier along the shoulder of the road. Then excitement started once again. From off to the left I began to hear dogs barking. This was followed by the ping of a bullet going past my head. Fortunately it went past, although in the state I was at that time, I don't think it would have made much difference if the bullet had penetrated. It was a rifle bullet—I knew that sound from my brother's hunting experiences—and I wanted to get away from there. I stood for a while trying to decide whether to go back to the car and chance a kind Samaritan coming along to help us, or just keep on going and hope for the best in the trenches. At that moment I was smitten on the head by an intense light. I looked up, but I could see nothing beyond the glare.

"You in trouble, lady?" a man's voice called from an invisible car.

"Yes, I am. I've just lost another tire."

"Reckon we can fix you up. How far is it?"

"I don't know, I really don't know. It's back that way on the right-hand shoulder—the left-hand shoulder the way you're going."

"Climb in, lady, and we'll take you back to it if you can recognize your car in the dark."

Gratefully, I fell into the back seat. And then I realized that all around me were bars. I was in the back seat of a paddy wagon. And in the back seat I triumphantly rode back to Lenore, driven by two state troopers, who were out, I suppose, to patrol the road. They said they were just "Seein' the sights."

At any rate, troopers are wonderful people. These changed and patched and poked to repair the tires, advised purchasing a whole new outfit of them in the next town, which was only a hundred miles away—good thing I didn't try to walk it—and saw us on our way, past the dogs, past the bullet-discharging rifle, past the cluster of houses that formed an unnamed settlement on the map, and so onward, upward, and over the mountains that loomed before us in the west.

We came down into the valley below the mountains, behind the mountains, and already I thought I could smell water. It was a grateful smell after the night we had been through, when everything had been bone dry. And with this cheery note, we limped up and down into the town of Riverside and beyond to the Sherman Institute, the local training school for Indian students.

I didn't know it at the time but that summer at the Sherman Institute was to shape much of the rest of my life, and still does. First, of course, there was Eric Douglas, a born teacher and a born reformer. Reform to him took the shape of enlightening the darkness and ignorance around him on the subject of Indian arts and crafts. Mr. Douglas was sitting on the front porch of the employees' quarters, and he looked at us from his full six feet four inches and said "You look as if you could do with some iced tea." I said yes, and my friend said no—she wanted a bath. So Eric and I spent the rest of the afternoon at the Riverside Inn consuming iced tea in unlimited quantities, and discussing in a vague kind of way the problems of Indian behavior.

Mabel Morrow was another field representive who shared Eric's interest and his enthusiasm, and a more incongruous pair of human beings I have never seen together. Mabel was tiny, not as tall as I am [5'6"], very thin at that time, with a mass of white hair piled and coiled in braids around her head. She had Siamese-cat blue eyes and a habit when she was deeply annoyed of projecting her lower lip in and out in a grimace that soon became known to all of us as the "Mabel face."

Mabel and Lenore got along. They had the "thing of the hands" in common. They enjoyed each other. Lenore was housed in the school dormitory, and I in the employees' club at the other end of the Sherman campus. Lenore took comfort in the thought that Mabel refused to live in anything but students' quarters. Besides, she said she had more room in there for the trappings she had brought with her from the Great Lakes, from the Northern Plains, from the Southwest, from anywhere and everywhere a train bound for Los Angeles would stop. Lenore learned how to spin, and all these were mysteries denied to me because I was a teacher and I had to teach other people.

Every night Lenore rehearsed for me her lesson of the day, and every night I dutifully committed it to memory and had something to lay before the students in the morning. In the employees' club the Arts and Crafts Board had what amounted to a wing of its own. Gladys Tantaquidgeon and I shared one room and a sleeping porch. Down the hall from us was first Eric, then René (Kenneth Fisher was not there because he was down visiting with his parents in Riverside itself), and Kenneth

Chapman, analyst, discoverer, and artist of Indian pottery in the Southwest. Other people came and went, but the five of us remained.

The first morning I sat at the breakfast table and looked across at Eric, whose head was bent on the end of his neck at a dangerously right-angled twist.

"What's the matter with you?" I asked, "Didn't you sleep well?"

"I did not," said Eric, and tried to turn his head. It wouldn't move. "I had the hardest, dirtiest, rockbound pillow under me that I have ever encountered."

"Well, you'd better get rid of it," I said. "Maybe the housekeeper has another one."

"I asked her. She doesn't."

"Well, then you'd better get used to it," I suggested.

"No, I don't think I could get used to that if the devil himself were standing over me. I couldn't get used to that pillow." I shrugged and continued with my mandatory government-issue oatmeal.

The next morning Eric was bright and chipper, his head upright at the top of his neck, smiling and beaming and happy as a lark. Apparently he had not slept on that pillow, but René, who came in a few minutes later with his head bent to the opposing angle that Eric's had taken, must have. He too complained of the pillow. And suddenly I realized what had happened. Eric, in some moment of desperation, tiptoed down the hall, removed the pillow from beneath René's head, inserted the rock, and returned to his now uninterrupted slumber. This was a very good thing for Eric and a very bad thing for René, who had more neck than most people. Eventually they realized what had happened and how all this had come about.

After much conclave in quarters they reached an agreement. Late that night, just before everyone turned in and the lights went out at the power house, René sallied forth from his room, carrying the offending pillow with him, reached Mr. Chapman's room, inserted the pillow, withdrew the one Chapman was using, and returned undetected to his own room.

The following morning, though, contrary to all previous indications, there were three upright men with straight, comfortable well-adjusted spines. Mr. Chapman had slept well? we asked. "Oh yes," he said. He had been perfectly comfortable, he was always comfortable. "A very restful bed, actually. Yes, oh yes." Yes, he noticed the pillow. "There was a pillow, wasn't there?" If we all said so there must have been, but—and he beamed on us in a fatherly way. "You know, dears, I never have slept on a pillow in my life. I always put them out of the bed and on the floor, if somebody puts one in."

End of pillows. Nobody ever referred to that episode again, except Mabel, Lenore, and me, and then only in the female privacy of a dining room in a Fred Harvey House.

So much was rolled into that one summer at Sherman that it is hard for me to determine the sequence after all these years. I know that we spent a weekend with René and the Dischers at Laguna Beach. Gladys, Mohegan Indian that she was, dark-skinned that she is, did not sunburn. I had red hair and the skin that matches it, and I did burn. In fact, I returned to the Institute with third-degree burns on arms and legs. René announced that I must go into the infirmary, but that was impossible because the infirmary was closed for the summer. Nobody but students could be expected to need an infirmary.

It ended with Kenneth Discher's producing a family doctor from Riverside who forthwith put me to bed in the employees' club, gave me strong, strong black tea in which to bathe, and told me to stay put except for getting up to sponge myself.

I know I spent four days in that room, I know that somebody (it must have been Kenneth) brought me enormous avocadoes and that I lived on them—anything else was too repulsive to contemplate. I know that I got up from my bed of pain and staggered with Gladys and Eric to see my very first grand opera, *Die Walküre*. I knew the music, but I had never seen it on stage. And when the lights went out in the Hollywood Bowl, the orchestra surged upward, and a stream of wild-haired Walkyries rode on white horses round the cliffs of the mountains that enclosed the bowl. Nobody was as excited or as frantically happy as I.

I remember the next day going with Gladys and Mr. Chapman into San Diego to see the zoo. For years I had heard of that zoo, and of the fact that it had the most complete collection of primates in captivity anywhere. It was exciting and a thrilling sight for an anthropologist to watch these remote cousins swinging from trees, branches, and trapezes, what have you, or simply wandering along the bars and moats of the cages in which they were confined. That zoo was all too human. I couldn't stand it. The thought of all those people locked up forever to be stared at by strangers was just too much. It hit home somehow. Maybe it was a forecast of what was to come to all the world in later years.

And I remember from that summer a multitude of people who came and went, particularly, of course, Maria Martinez and Julián, her husband. They became my friends, I became theirs, and of all the demonstrators and instructors who came to Sherman Institute that summer, they were the most interesting and the most attractive that I knew.

3

THE WAY SHE WAS: MARIA

NOTHING IN THE WORLD comes free. That is particularly true when you have known a person of fame and distinction. In my own case, that person is Maria Martinez, a potter of San Ildefonso Pueblo. The price demanded of me in her case is that I tell ALL, everything I know about Maria as a person.

That is a little hard to do for several reasons. In the first place I wrote a book about Maria. (*Maria: The Potter of San Ildefonso*, 1948) That was forty years ago, and a lot of water has gone down the Rio Grande and past San Ildefonso since then. Maria has passed to a reward one can only hope is worthy of her. Time has gone by. Nothing is, or ever will be again, quite as it was when Maria and I sat on the adobe floor of her living room, with a long table covered with polished black ware behind us, and talked and talked and talked.

Maria Martinez Finishing One of Her Pots at San Ildefonso Pueblo.
Courtesy University of Oklahoma, Norman, Oklahoma, n.d., Photo #525

Time and the river notwithstanding, Maria is as clear in my mind now as she was in those long ago spring mornings. It is always Spring when I think of Maria, although two years went into the recording of her memories. Fall and winter seem to have disappeared into the blaze of midsummer. It is always Spring. The apricot trees are laden with blossoms, as later, we hope, they will be laden with fruit. The men are coming and going along the ditch that edges the field outside. They are preparing to open the gates and let the water through clean channels and across fields. Much of our talking at these times of spring mornings is accompanied by the gentle seething of simmering pots of posole and chile con carne, and underlain with the perfume of fresh bread baking in the oven by the kitchen door.

Somewhere in the distance, down inside the Kiva, the older men are singing, and the thud of the accompanying drums comes to us, mixed with voices. Yes, it is Spring. Next Sunday it will be Easter, and already the palm branches, given to the women at the end of the Palm Sunday service, are curling a little against the chimney. And on Saturday, Holy Saturday, the men will all sing as they raise the ditch gates, and the women will sing as they come from their houses with the bowls and loaves of fresh-cooked food. And on Monday, after the Easter dance, Maria and I will resume our talking as if nothing had happened.

Maria Martinez with Alice Marriott Taking Field Notes at San Ildefonso Pueblo. Courtesy University of Oklahoma, Norman, Oklahoma, n.d., Photo #546

"Maria," I say, with the endless poking and prodding of the social scientist, "What did that first potsherd look like? The one Julián picked up from the ground, in the fallen-down house on the Pajarito Plateau? The one he and Dr. Hewett [Edgar Hewett, PhD] brought to you to copy?"

Maria's round face curls upward as she thinks about that long past spring.

"It was *PREtty*," she says. "Very *pretty*. Little fine black line on white. They followed the shape of the bowl. Curved with it, as if the bowl shaped them. Very hard ware, too. Harder than we make nowadays. It had to be hard. Peoples eat out of it. It was used. I could still see the grease stains from the meat in the posole."

"Doesn't that still happen? The stains?"

"No-o-o." Maria seemed reluctant to let go of the thought of that ancient bowl. "Nowadays the puttries is soft. The grease soaks into them and you can't see it. Look, I show that potsherd. I put it away in the wall somewheres."

Most older Pueblo women have that custom. They chop a hole in the adobe wall with a hatchet, lay the treasure—whatever it may be—in the hole, and then cover the hole and its contents with a smear of adobe. The work is neatly done, for the women do all the plaster work in and on their houses; it is not men's work, they say. Soon, unless a picture has covered the trove, or a tiny pile of mud has hardened where it fell to the floor, there is no clue to the hiding place.

So it was not surprising to see Maria rise, leave the room for the wood pile, and return clasping a hatchet. She took down the print of San Ildefonso writing poetry to the Virgin and the Virgin politely thanking him for it, and gave the wall beneath the print a resounding whack with her hatchet. A small neat piece of dry adobe fell to the floor at Maria's feet, but nothing else happened.

"Well!" said Maria. "Looks like that potsherd don't want to come out!"

"It must feel right at home," I ventured.

"It gots to come out," Maria declared. "Been there too long, thinks it belong there. We get you, though," she addressed the invisible potsherd, and whacked the wall mightily for a second time.

"Let me try," I offered, and Maria surrendered the hatchet into my hands.

I moved a little to the right, closer to the place where the margin of the picture frame had hung, and whacked in my turn. Again a piece of hard dry adobe. Nothing else. The potsherd eluded me as it had Maria.

"Must like it in there," Maria suggested, and took her turn at the whacking.

Together, between us, we pecked holes in most of the wall's surface. No potsherd. The wall looked as if it would need replastering.

"Could you draw it?" I queried, when we both paused for breath.

"I guess," Maria seemed less enthusiastic about drawing than she had about cutting holes in the wall. "That's a man's work though. Julián, he always do that. Maybe he don't want me to find it. He play joke on us. He always playing joke."

That seemed a little farfetched, even for Julián. True, he had had a keen sense of humor. But was it likely to have survived the six years since his death in 1943?

"You remember him joking," Maria was insistent. "In San Francisco? All us ladies standing around, waiting for the World's Fair salesroom to open. Just talking a little to each other?"

My mind flashed back to the salesroom in the Government Building of the Pan Pacific Exposition. We were all there, Indian demonstrators and Anglo employees alike, to show an eager public what Indians could do with the arts when they had a chance and minimal interference.

The ladies clumped, shyly, and talked quietly, while the men clustered, and spread apart, ever curious to look at the great structure that housed their wares. Out of the men's group, suddenly, Julián came dancing. Tied firmly over his face was a mask of braided corn husk, the face of a pig, such as the Senecas wear in their midwinter False Face Society dances. At its mildest the effect above Julián's red-brown calf-high moccasins, silk shirt and matching breech clout, and neatly braided, gray-tinged black hair, would have been grotesque anywhere. In these surroundings, it was more so—laughable to a degree.

"I catch you yet!" Julián was singing a Forty-Nine Dance song, an intertribal possession. With one hand he grabbed the arm of a Cheyenne beadworker and with the other caught hold of a Papago basketmaker, and the three circled in a shuffling circle before us. "I got you now!" Julián yelled triumphantly. He let go of his first two partners and seized a Navajo weaver and a Sioux tanner. "We go fine!" he observed.

Three times they circled around us, but on the fourth turn, Julián released the Sioux and reached for me.

"I get me a Anglo," he triumphed.

In those days I was younger than I am now, and much, much thinner. With a flip of the hips I eluded Julián's outstretched hand, and dropped behind the Navajo lady, out of reach. "She gets away from me," Julián wailed full-voiced. "Always the way with them Anglos." In a straggling line of three, the basketmaker doubled up with laughter from where she watched. We made the circuit again, and this time I dropped away and crouched beside Maria. She in her turn, grasped her husband's outreaching hand—a maneuver unknown in the Forty-Nine—and smacked me on the bottom with her free palm, roaring with laughter, like everyone else. Unnoticed by us, the doors of the salesroom had opened and shoppers had begun to straggle in.

"Get away from my man, you Anglo," Maria commanded. Then, having disposed of me she smacked Julián on the bottom, too, and marched with massive dignity to her working place.

The group fell apart, like filings when a magnet is laid down, and the day's work began.

That was the beginning of a long and rewarding—for me—friendship. Or, rather, of two. My relations with Maria became those of an older and younger sister. With Julián, however friendly we became, there was always a gap, as there must be between a man and a woman who have flirted publicly.

So in the room with the pockmarked walls, Maria and I sat comfortably, companionably, and thought back to the man who had amused and shocked and often delighted us. Julián was gone.

In the old Pueblo fashion, he had chosen his burial place soon after puberty—a clean wind-swept clearing among the junipers of the Pajarito Plateau. His resting place was unmarked and was known only to Maria and their sons. But from the clearing Julián could watch over all of us, his immortal mouth twisted in a smile, as long as we needed and remembered him.

Remembered him! Who that had known Julián could forget him?

We remembered a time when the senior class was graduating from the Indian High School in Santa Fe. This was to be a great occasion, with all available parents and *primos* assembled. Tony, the third son, who was later known as Po-Povi-Da, which translates as The Red Fox, was class president. Maria as a moulder, almost a sculptor, of pottery, and Julián as painter-decorator, were just coming into recognition as artists. It behooved them to do their son honor.

Julián Martinez Decorating Pots at San Ildefonso Pueblo. Courtesy University of Oklahoma, Norman, Oklahoma, n.d., Photo #547

"What dress shall I wear?" Maria asked Po, as any mother might ask her son. She was thinking of the printed cotton *mantas* hanging in her cupboard. They were all, she thought, equally beautiful.

"I buy you a dress," Po said. "I saw one down town that would look good on you."

He came home that evening with a box under his arm, which he kept hidden from Maria until the day before Graduation Day.

"How can I make a dress when I don't see the goods?" Maria queried.

"You don't have to make it. It's already made. You'll see." That was the end of that.

Po left the night before graduation to be on hand at the school in the morning. Early, when she was sure he was gone, Maria found and opened the box. The dress inside was folded neatly and securely in white tissue paper. Maria shook it out of the wrappings and into its drapery. She sat down on the bed and gasped.

She had seen pictures of such dresses before. An Anglo woman's evening dress! The green velvet draped softly across her outstretched arm and fell richly almost to her moccasins. The bottom, with its flowing skirt, was all right. But the top! A scooped out neck—low, low. Straps over the shoulders, no sleeves. The color was beautiful and the goods were fine, but this dress would leave her bare naked. It would show off the parts of her body a pueblo woman never reveals.

Maria had never been in a hospital, not even to have a baby. She had borne her sons at home, with her mother and sisters in attendance. Not even Julián had seen her bare shoulders and throat. This dress was a scandal.

And yet—it had been Po's proud gift. He, of all the boys, most wanted her to look beautiful, and—and...Maria could not summon the word "smart," but she was thinking it. Finally, her mouth set, she slipped out of her cotton *manta*. True, that *manta* left her right shoulder bare. One was as bad as two—almost. Gravely, seriously, she let the velvet slip over her body. Po would be pleased and proud. If she wore a blanket—her new green-striped Pendleton, perhaps—the green velvet would show at the bottom, and Po would know she had his dress on. There would be no hurt feelings for him, or for anybody.

She dressed, wrapped the blanket around her, and took her place beside Julián in the wagon seat.

"Aren't you hot in that?" he asked, fingering the blanket's wool.

"I'm all right."

"I'll go back and get you a light shawl."

"I'm all right. Let's get started. We might be late."

They were right on time. The students were forming a line of dark red robes and flat caps with tassels, to march into the auditorium. Maria slipped past them into the reserved seats on the aisle Po had marked with their names. They sat for a moment, then stood, while the procession filed past them. Po led the others, and his forehead was creased with a frown until he looked down at his mother's feet. She still wore moccasins, for lack of other footgear, but the green velvet showed brightly above the red-dyed leather.

There was singing. Papers were read. The Principal, the Superintendent of Education, the Indian Agent—each made a speech. Prizes were presented. The tassels were moved from one side of the flat caps to the other. Another song. It was over and the students were filing out and scattering into groups as they reached the door.

"Come on," Julián urged. "We eat in the cafeteria, they say. I'm hungry."

Po was before him, seizing his mother's arm. "The Commissioner is here," he informed them. "He wants to meet you."

"I'd rather meet the cook," said Julián. Maria jabbed him in the ribs with her elbow.

"We meet the Commissioner," she said, gazing at Po, who led them out of the crowd and to a group of Anglos, who had gathered under the shade of the trees.

"Mr. Commissioner," said the Class President, every inch of him standing straight, "This is my mother, Maria Martinez, and my father, Julián."

A short, rather rosy Anglo man bowed to Maria and shook hands with Julián.

"I know your pottery," he said. "I've admired it for a long time. My wife has some of it. I told her that if I met you, and had a chance, I'd ask you to make her a piece."

"Takes a long time," Maria hazarded. "Maybe I make it after we go home."

"I'd like to see it made," the Commissioner pressed. "Tell her I saw it from start to finish."

"I got my good dress on. Putteries is muddy to make. My NEW dress," she insisted. "Po gave it to me."

"Well, I'm sure he'd like a picture of his mother in the dress," the Commissioner smiled at her boy. It was hopeless. A thought came to Maria from nowhere. "Take your father to the kitchen and have the cook fill him up," she said in Tewa. "And please get her to lend me an apron. I don't want to get this dress dirty."

Julián and Po disappeared and Po was back with a long white coverall apron, before Maria could catch her breath. She turned slightly away from the men, slid the apron neck strings over her head, and tied the other strings around her waist under the blanket. The blanket slid to the ground, Po picked it up. He beamed at his mother, proudly.

"You look beautiful in that," he said.

"Thank you for the dress," Maria replied.

Someone had brought a worktable and a chair for her. Younger students brought her a gunnysack filled with mud. Po gazed at her, pride and confusion mingling on his face. Maria seated herself behind the table and went to work. She patted out a clay tortilla as Tía Nicolasa had taught her to do, long ago, when she and her sisters were little girls in the pueblo. It was almost as if Tía Nicolasa were standing beside her, encouraging her for a moment. Gravely, Maria shaped the tortilla so its sides curved upward, and the base of the bowl took shape. She and Tía Nicolasa were alone again, absorbed in their work, as they had often been. Then it was over. The bowl was shaped and formed. She smiled at the Commissioner: "That wonderful grin," as someone once had called it.

"I take it home to fire it," Maria said. "Too wet now. We send it to you for your wife." She shook out her skirt as if it had been cotton, not velvet. She took off her apron and turned to Po. "I wear your dress," she said, not at all ashamed by her near nakedness.

"Come get your lunch. You must be hungry, too," her son said, and they went together to the kitchen where the girls were cleaning up—all but three places at one end of the worktable, where the Martinez family sat for their meal. Only Julián had even a slightly diminished appetite, and he stared at Maria as if he had never seen her before.

There was a silence in the room for a moment, and then Maria turned to me.

"I remember now," she said. "Julián, he tell me. NOT this room, the kitchen, because that's where he always find me if he want me."

She led the way into the next room and took down a picture of San Isidro, the farmer. Behind it there was the slightest indentation in the wall. There Maria unerringly struck with the hatchet. A sheet of adobe, not bonded to the rest of the wall, dropped to the floor. Behind it, in the wall, was a little heap of potsherds. Maria picked up one.

"This is it," she said with surety, and handed the fragment to me. Black lines against a white slip lay in my palm, curving upward as the clay curved.

"Beautiful," I said.

"That what Julián say," Maria answered. "Too beautiful to lose."

I have known a lot of people in my comings and goings. It is hard, sometimes, to sort things out. But there is no chance of confusing Maria or Julián with anyone else—not even with any other Tewa. They stand, alone and complete with each other: artists, workers, parents, and friends, and they can never be confused with anyone else.

4

IN AND AROUND
NEW MEXICO

AS I HAVE SAID BEFORE, I was not drawn to New Mexico. I was <u>hurled</u> into New Mexico on the trip to Riverside, California, in 1938 to teach anthropology at the Sherman Institute. On the trip back to Oklahoma, Lenore Sloan and I stopped in New Mexico because Eric Douglas had told us that on the Fourth of August, one neat little month after we had encountered him at Flagstaff, the pueblo of Santo Domingo would be holding its annual Corn Dance. I didn't know it then, but I've since learned, that this is one of the great and spectacular religious observances of the Southwest. Indians come from all over the area to put on their own arts and crafts show, which is much different from the arts and crafts shows that had been put on in museums prior to that time.

Everybody who had anything to sell sat in the shade of the cottonwoods along the bank of the acequia, his or her—more usually her—possessions spread out before her. And tourists, locals, Indians from other groups, anybody and everybody who happened to be in New Mexico at that time wandered along the meandering stream and <u>acquired</u>. I do mean acquired, because in those days you could buy a beautiful Santo Domingo meal bowl for two dollars. I still have it, and it's one of the handsomest I have ever seen. It was made by one of a family of distinguished potters, one of the Aquilaf sisters, a blood member of that family, not a clan sister. It was the first time I realized that you could tell the work of one potter from the work of another.

The next time I was drawn to New Mexico was at the behest of the greatest mother, the American Red Cross, which had hired me in 1942 as a field representative. I was assigned to Southwest Texas—the area of the Guadalupe Mountains, San Antonio, everything in between, including Fort Davis, the calvary post. The area was a good mouthful, slightly larger than New England, and I found that I got tired. More than that, I was zigzagging across the border, because many of the people in the armed services had been born in Mexico, their families were there, and my job was to talk to families, to organize local Red

Cross chapters that would do the work for me, and generally keep the Red Cross in touch with the people in the outlying districts.

It finally got to be too much, and I asked for a slightly smaller territory, which turned out to be everything in New Mexico between the Arizona line and the east-bound Rio Grande, and from Mexico north to Colorado. It was smaller geographically, I will say that. It was also densely populated, but the greatest Mother and I rocked along through famine, fire, and flood—to put it mildly.

I think always of Reserve, New Mexico, a county seat without public transportation, telephone lines, paved streets, a hotel, a restaurant, any of the mild amenities that one usually finds in county seats. Reserve became a little frustrating and tiring when you had fifteen feet of snow on the flat, and you had to get out to the next chapter, which was in Silver City, ninety-five miles down the road and over the mountain.

They used to say in Reserve that first the Forest Service car went through, then the highway patrol car went through, and then the Red Cross limped along down in the background. We got through though, and I will say that I took third place to the men, because they wouldn't let me go first. Of course, I couldn't dig as well as they could. But we did get there, and that was a sensation, an occupation, and an experience that I wish I could forget.

My first impressions of the Southwest, New Mexico in particular, have been overlaid with so many other impressions, and I can't keep track of all of them. The country was beautiful, the sky was high and clear and blue, the mountains at their best were most gorgeous. Snow in the days when I first went there lasted on the high peaks until almost the first of June, and renewed itself in early October. So we used to use Truchas mountain, which was visible from the front door, as a sort of barometer and we could pretty well predict the weather from the clouds or clearness around its peak.

Ruggedness I expected. That went without saying. It was beautiful country, it was magnificent country, it was gigantic country, and aside from experiencing a few frights over height, which I managed to bring under control, it was superb country. I loved it.

Santa Fe in and of itself in those days was dusty, dry, very rough underfoot, filled usually with people whose language I did not understand too well at the time, but who were willing to grin at me if I grinned back. We all got along with everybody pretty well.

The influx of *turistas* was not overwhelming before the end of World War II. When the bombs fell on Hiroshima and Nagasaki, they knocked out a lot of culture that had existed in New Mexico previously. It would not be too much to say that the greatest changes in Santa Fe as a town began in 1941, when the

Manhattan Project at Los Alamos was instigated, and afterwards activated.

Los Alamos had been a school on the Pajarito Plateau, a very exclusive boys boarding school run by some extraordinary and gifted people who sacrificed school and plateau forever at the behest of the government. Immediately thereafter the population of Santa Fe proper increased at least a thousand fold, and all of these newcomers were crammed into one post office box— number 1620. Babies were born, dinners were given, funerals were conducted from that container, because nobody could have any other civilian address. It was a wild and wonderful time, and driving up the plateau—it is still indescribable.

Santa Fe grew from a meager population of 20,000 in the entire county to its near 100,000 today. Bruns Hospital, which was opened south of the city as an army reclamation project, you might say, increased the civilian and military population of the area considerably.

Santa Fe was the town where we went to do the shopping. If the roads south were too bad we went to Española on the north branch of the Taos road. Santa Fe was the place that had the public library. It had two very good dress shops in the forties. It accommodated the state penitentiary, and it was just a small town. As an anthropologist, and later as a field representative for the Red Cross, I was used to small towns. They didn't just hit me in the eye the way they seem to do some people.

I liked the fact that Santa Fe was the oldest city in the United States, and proudly insists that it still is. I liked the Palace of the Governors, which has been the home of territorial governors and for a time of statehood governors. It had been an administrative building, too. And it had just been converted into a kind of museum of the Aunt Martha's attic type, but the museum was coming along.

The plaza had the usual layout of Spanish-American territorial towns. I've seen them in Mexico, very similar—the barracks on one side, the chapel on the other. By the time I got to Santa Fe, however, you could never have identified the chapel as a chapel, because it had become a set of stores.

The most important things about it showed up later. The oldest house in the United States stood on College Street, six blocks from the plaza. The oldest church adjoined it. There was enough construction layered underground to keep an indefinite number of archeologists busy, and some of it still does. But for the ethnologists it was the population and the people who were most attractive, interesting.

When I arrived in New Mexico to begin a biography of Maria Martinez at San Ildefonso Pueblo, I rented a house from friends. San Ildefonso then was an extremely narrow-minded pueblo, as it is now, and Anglos were not included in its population in any way. To work at San Ildefonso I had to live either in Santa Fe proper or near it in what we always called "the valley." The valley population turned out to be composed of the then defunct pueblo of Pojoaque, which because it exists on paper in government records, the other pueblos have a sand bed from which to take their tempering materials for pottery.

Then there was Nambe Spanish Town, centering around the Church of Corazon Sagrado and beyond that Nambe Pueblo, which is the only one remaining of the seven Indian pueblos that had surrounded the valley in the 1500s.

I rented a little mud pie of a house for $5 a month, and that figure gives you a pretty good comparison of what things were worth then and now, forty-odd years later. You couldn't buy an inch of ground in Nambe Valley now for $5. But then I could rent a house with a well—sort of—for $5 a month. We didn't have electricity and we didn't have an electric pump, so all our water had to be carried. We had only kerosene lanterns, but that was true in town and in a lot of other sections.

Nambe had no post office. Nambe obviously couldn't have a post office. There were maybe a dozen people in the valley all told, and we didn't need a post office. We got rural delivery from Santa Fe. Our address was Santa Fe. We didn't live in Santa Fe, but that was our address for postal purposes.

I fell in love with the valley, and I'm still in love with the valley as I remember it. Not as it is now, full of ramshackle, rag-tagged, bobtailed "modren" architecture that is pretty plain horrible. But nice old solid adobe houses that hug the earth were architecture enough for living purposes. I learned to plaster the houses on the outside and the inside with fresh adobe once a year. You could learn a great many things in Nambe at that time that didn't even touch your existence anywhere else. And it was like stepping back almost to the 1700s.

Nambe was a magnificent place and it did have a road that went from the town along the acequias and the Pojoaque Wash to San Ildefonso, where the Pojoaque Wash joined hands with the Rio Grande to become the north and south flowing river that we know today. It was a beautiful and a strange and a most wonderful place to live. Anything you see or hear about it now has nothing to do with the valley as I knew it.

It was in Nambe that I first met José de la Cruz de Romero. José de la Cruz, Joseph of Aramathia, is the first name—Christian name—of the man. He was always called Cruz, to distinguish him from the innumerable other José Romeros scattered around Santa Fe County. I knew him as Cruz, and in *The Valley Below* I wrote of him as Maclovio Salazar simply because I liked the name. It was the name of Cruz's son-in-law, and I liked the sound of it, and it was almost unidentifiable.

Cruz represented the Indian and Spanish population elements, but not the Anglo in any sense of the word. Nowadays, "Hispanic" means one thing and "Anglo" another, and both are parts of what social scientists have come to refer to as "ethnic consciousness." That there was ever a time when the words were no more than handy means of identification, not of value judgements expressed or implied, is almost forgotten. In the days when I lived in the valley, there were no such value judgements. There were men and women of different backgrounds, but one background was no more valuable than another. Each was equal. Each was valid.

Cruz and I lived as neighbors and worked as friends in the valley below the Sangre de Cristo Mountains. During those years, he taught me many things: to work with my hands and enjoy the health and strength that made work possible; to build a fire and clean a wood stove; to plant alfalfa—he always said "arfarfa"—and to find someone who would harvest it; to cook for a ditch crew and to feed a visiting tribal council with the same formality that one showed to a visiting dignitary of church or state.

Above all, he told me of the saints of the villages and the pueblos, as if they were real men and women. To him, they were. I am not a Roman Catholic, but I came to respect and admire and laugh at and cry with his friends the saints: San Miguel (Saint Michael), whom God ordered to run Satan out of Heaven "like he's a bool in the arfarfa field." Or San Juan Bautista (Saint John the Baptist), who was charged by God the Father "to take Tía Maria's son to the reever Jordan, and pour water on his head three times, and give him the name Jesus."

It was as a teacher that Cruz told the stories of the

saints to me. He was a good teacher. The proof of that is that I have remembered the stories, as he told them, for almost half a lifetime, even to the flow and lilt of his voice. That he never made a Roman Catholic of me is beside the point. He taught me that men and women of whatever faith can transcend the pettiness of their surroundings, and rise above them to the feet of God.

I also have vivid memories of the annual pilgrimage that the Bataan prisoners of war made to the Santuario de Chimayó— the Sanctuary of the Holy Child of Prague. During the time the young New Mexico men were in service and were captured by the Japanese, many of them who were Roman Catholics pledged themselves to make an annual pilgrimage to the shrine of the Infant of Prague, the Lost Child, if he brought them home. They, and the veterans of more recent wars, still make this Easter Pilgrimage to Chimayó.

They came on that first Easter in 1946 from all over New Mexico, those who could move or be moved. They formed a moving mass up the back roads. They didn't try to take the highways in those days. Nowadays the state patrol comes out and stops other traffic until the veterans have gone by. But in the 40s they were all young, young, young, and they liked the back country anyhow. And they went by its dirt roads. I heard about this through the grapevine, via Cruz, and decided that I would go and take part in it. Maybe I would see some of these men whose mothers I had been working with during the war, and perhaps, just possibly, get some photographs. I didn't get any photographs. You couldn't photograph a moving caterpillar of men, some in cars (they couldn't walk), some in wheelchairs, many on crutches, some with artificial limbs—all of them attended by weeping and singing families as they covered the roads from the Mexican border northward to Chimayó, which is just above Nambe.

I drove to Española where the road into Chimayó Valley turned off to the east, and there I left my car and walked with the others. I still can't talk about this without crying. And one of the things I remember hearing was one veteran saying to an old man: "Who is that Anglo woman and why is she here with us?" And the old man replying: "Quiet, my son, she has a right."

And that is about as much as I remember of the first pilgrimage. Of course, there have been pilgrimages ever since. Nowadays the veterans come from discharge in Vietnam, even Korea. Many of them now have served without combat in the European theatre, but they come, even those who were in the Middle East. They still make the pilgrimage, and it is still an immensely moving thing to see. Its length is shortened. People join it at Santa Fe or at Española now, because it's just too far to go by back roads from the Mexican border, but the pilgrimage still takes place. A grotto has been built behind the Santuario, where Mass is held on high holidays, including, of course, Easter.

I wasn't there this year [1987]; I didn't get to see it. I don't know whether I could have walked more than a hundred yards myself, but I would have tried if I had been able to get there.

5

DISTINGUISHED ANGLO FRIENDS

I AM REMINDED of two people: one is Mabel Dodge Luhan; the other is Oliver La Farge. Mabel Luhan was no more an ordinary woman than Oliver was an ordinary man. They had one great thing in common. They were fascinated with their own interpretation of the universe as it revolved around them.

Mabel Luhan was far from an ordinary woman. Her six-volume autobiography is nothing to sneeze at, unless it has been coated with dust. I think it will be read for a great many years because it picks up the never-never land in which Mabel Luhan dwelt, whether the other occupants welcomed or enjoyed her or not, or whether or not they sympathized with her approach to life.

Oliver La Farge, on the other hand, was concerned with the hows and the whys of everything; it was all grist to his mill. He was always and perpetually fascinated by the behavior of human creatures around him.

Thinking of Mabel Luhan again, I am reminded of her majestic indifference to the public opinion of the Taos Pueblo and all the other people in Taos County. She came there, she settled there, she saw the man with whom she wished to end her days, and she joined his life to hers to the best of her ability, which was considerable. She had honed her talents on the IWW (Industrial Workers of the World) and other groups of reformers, and on the then current (1920s) New York scene.

Oliver I knew best in the last years of his life. He introduced me to many new forms of European art. Beautiful they are and striking, and the colors used—blues, greens, yellows, and whites—are pleasant and soothing. But the thing that keeps me coming back to M. Matisse cutouts, for instance, is the strong resemblance to the cutout paper patterns made by certain Indian tribes—by the women of those tribes particularly.

And then there was Mary Wheelwright, in whose historic home I lived the last two summers before her death, in 1958 at the age of eighty. I was very happy, very lucky that Mary let me stay at Los Luceros, her beautiful home in Alcalde, New Mexico, five miles north of Espanola. Mary's overseer and my longtime friend Maria Chabot convinced Mary that here was this pitiful child wasting away in a hospital and that she would be much better off at Los Luceros. So they swooped down and removed me from the hospital. I had had surgery and I was weak and a very useless kind of creature, so Mary took me up to Los Luceros. That was the first time I ever stayed there, although I had visited the place with Dorothy Stewart and people who had really discovered Santa Fe in the twenties, and had made it quite a place in the thirties and even into the forties. But I really don't know why Mary let me stay. I was not, in a sense, her cup of tea, except that I had an English father.

I was still under my doctor's supervision when one morning I drove into town to get groceries. I came back to find Mary and Dr. Michael Pijoan pacing up and down the second floor gallery. Mary was going east and Dr. Pijoan was going west, and they would encounter each other in the middle.

I heard Mary boom—and she could boom! "It's no use trying to argue with me, young man. You've filled that child so full of pills she clanks when she walks!" I've never seen Dr. Pijoan stopped in his tracks by anybody the way he was by Mary. In the exact middle of the gallery they turned side by side, walked through the sala, down the stairs, and Mary threw the front door open and said, "Good day!" And off he went.

Mary Wheelwright was a big woman—about five feet ten, which was tall in that age. I was five feet six, and she towered over me. She was big-boned, with one of those craggy New

England faces. After all, she was a Cabot and a Wheelwright of Boston, and you don't expect them to look like other people. She didn't. In her own way she was a very handsome woman. She had masses of beautifully curly dark brown hair, which was turning gray when I knew her.

Mary's weekly trip into Santa Fe included a stopover at the Sena Plaza Beauty Parlor, where one of the beauticians would give her a shampoo and sit her down in front of the mirror and comb every blessed bit of curl out of that hair with a curling iron. I don't know how Mary stood it.

Mary dressed in Harris tweeds and tailored blouses. Very solid shoes. Down-sitting and up-standing she was. She had two hats. She had a beautiful fedora, the kind that is just coming into fashion again now, and a riding hat. She would wear one or the other as the occasion demanded. She rode a great deal. She loved horses, and she rode sidesaddle. She wouldn't ride astride. And I used to be allowed to go riding with Mary, because I too rode sidesaddle. My father came out from England with the firm conviction that a lady didn't straddle a horse.

I do remember about dressing up the time that she had invited me to lunch at the Cosmopolitan Club in New York, which is an exclusive woman's club. I had gotten myself dressed to the nines in a black crepe tailored dress and a beautifully fitted black coat. It was a Schiaparelli. I had done some modeling for the lady, and she couldn't pay a government employee in money, but she had given me this beautiful coat, and a friend had loaned me a Gainsboroughlike sweeping black hat with a feather. I wore it to the Cosmopolitan Club, and I looked around for the familiar Harris tweed, and there wasn't a Harris tweed in sight. Finally I spotted a majestic vision in black and went over. As I approached she stood up and she said, "Alice, my dear, it's so good to see you." She threw her arms around me and hugged me and I think it was the only time Mary demonstrated affection for anybody. Then we sat there and laughed, because neither of us ever expected the other to be dressed up.

Mary had many friends. She was a friend of Laura Gilpin. The only really beautiful photograph of her I've seen, Laura took. And of course, Betsy Foster, who was Laura's companion for many years. Margaretta Dietrich and Dorothy Stewart, the two sisters. She knew many people in Santa Fe, but they were all carved out of the same block of granite, more or less. Mary Austin she knew. Helen Wood Stevens, whose husband had been the re-creator of the Shakespearean theatre in New York. And there were people who had been active in the arts at one time or another, and in one way or another. Her friend Lily Pons had bought a place in Taos, and she used to drive down and visit Mary every once in a while. She had such a magnificent bosom, and she would look at Mary and say, "This is what makes it easy, this!" You could never get Madame Pons to admit that her voice was in her throat; it was in her chest!

That was a close circle, very close. Very wonderful people, very generous, very kindhearted, everything that you could ask people to be. But they stayed to themselves. They were not people who would ordinarily mix with newcomers, or with latecomers even, unless they were properly introduced.

Mary was not a person who was a worrier, or a hypochondriac. I know that she had been one as a girl, but for how long I don't know. She had guests for dinner one evening, and after the meal the gentleman took out what looked like a snuffbox. On one side were his pills, and on the other side were his wife's pills, and they passed this thing back and forth and took their pills in turn. Mary watched this performance. She had a bell on the table, made by a Navajo. (It was supposed to show a portrait of Hostiin Klah, the esteemed Navajo medicine man and artist who collaborated with Mary in establishing in 1937 what has now become the Wheelwright Museum of the American Indian. But instead of depicting Klah with blankets clinging to his body from the waist down, the etched garment flared out like a woman's skirt.) That evening Mary rose up from the table, took the bell in her hand, and clanged it once. She said very quietly, "Now I'm sure you want to go home before your sleeping pills take effect." And they went.

There were not many sweet, endearing things that you can say about Mary. It wasn't like Mary Austin sitting in the middle of the garden on Camino del Sol, in among the flowers, and brushing that magnificent white hair. Mary Austin said once to a friend that weeds were all right, "they're just flowers growing in the wrong place. I like them."

Of course, there was not a weed in Mary Wheelwright's garden. Everything was done as precisely as it must have been done about 1830 or so, when her mother was a young woman. Mary was an only child. Her father died when she was quite young, and she and her mother made the team. I think she did love her mother, she certainly tolerated her. Mrs. Wheelwright was dead long before I knew Mary. She was on her own, but she didn't mind it. She was really like the spirit of old New England. I've known two or three other women who had that same quality. The one I know is in her eighties, and she is a very beautiful and dainty woman—Alice Everett in Oklahoma City. Every once in a while she says something that reminds me of Mary. They, too, were tarred with the same brush. I used that expression when Mary, Maria Chabot, and I were talking about a trading post at San Juan—how old it was, at least as old as Los Luceros. When I said that the men of both places must have been tarred with the same brush, Mary whooped with delight because she hadn't heard that expression for years. And Maria had never heard it at all, because she had come from San Antonio. Her life was all in the middle of the country.

Maria Chabot was a great influence in persuading Mary to establish orchards at Los Luceros. Maria planted the first prune plums on the land, which had twenty-five or thirty out of a total of one hundred acres under cultivation. There were apples and pears, apricots, nectarines, and peaches. I will never get over the smell of those peaches, because when the truckers came down the highway from Colorado they would stop at Los Luceros and pick up a load. All the crates had to be laid out, and I was the tally man. I would stand by that scale until I had to sit down on the floor of the truck. And I could not bear the smell of peaches for years.

But it was not all work. We would occasionally take off in Mary's magnificent old car—a Chrysler. It was the biggest blasted thing on four wheels. It was fitted with one of the first automatic shift drives, but it also had a hand shift in case you got into trouble. Mary would take care of the contingencies. Once, we started out for Taos. It was a nice day. She never drove her car herself. She had a chauffeur. But this day I drove, and we went to lunch at La Dona Luz—the restaurant—and Dorothy Brett came in and joined us. It was a lovely luncheon for me. People seemed to either dislike Brett or like her very much. Mary liked her. She could be amusing. She just got her first in-the-ear hearing aid with the battery and sound box on her chest, and she was showing it off to everyone. She practically undressed to display it. Until then she had used an ear trumpet, but this was new and real and wonderful, and Brett was very happy with it.

I have been asked many times about how Mary got her

house. I don't know how she got to New Mexico. I suspect that it was the same way as most of us got there—through friends. At that time, in the early twenties, Burton Staples had a dude ranch at Coolidge, New Mexico, in McKinley County. Many people used to go there—Judge and Mrs. William Denman, Mr. and Mrs. C. D. Elkins, Harold Ickes and the first Mrs. Ickes, Margaretta S. Dietrich, Malvina Hoffman, Dorothy Stewart, Madame Ernestine Schumann-Heink, Mary Wheelwright, John Evans (Mabel Dodge Luhan's son) to name a few. These were all people who had an interest in the Indians. It was a gathering place for people who were Indian lovers, and Indian art lovers. Mary entertained graciously. She was a founding mother of the WCTU and very much opposed to spirits, but not to wine, because wine was a food. We had a noonday dinner, usually with a bottle of white wine standing on the table, and Mary poured. She did that as correctly as she did everything else—sipping a sample in a glass, then pouring for the guests. Nothing extravagant in wine, of course. It was usually a sauterne.

As for Los Luceros, the house had been built after Oñate's Entrada. That dates it back to the 1720s. At that time it was only one story. The walls on the first floor are four feet thick, so that they accommodate wonderful window seats, but actually there weren't any windows at that time in the house anywhere.

It was divided by a long central hall, with the dining room opening out on the lake and the bosqué. The room used as a utility room was on the left. You came in the front door and were confronted, at the time I was familiar with it, by a great big oil heater. It was very efficient, too. It had to be in that place.

The house as originally built had served as an outpost for the Spanish troopers. They covered the territory as far north as Alamosa, within the upper range of the Sangre de Cristo and Jemez mountains, and the whole country was alive and growing (so said the occupants) with Apaches and Navajos. It was held as a fortress until after our war with Mexico. When that war ended, General Stephen Watts Kearny came into Santa Fe and became a military governor for a while. He left one of his colonels in charge of this upper territory. Rio Arriba County it was, even then.

The colonel happened to be a Mississippian. He looked the place over and it looked kind of sparse and dull, and he had plenty of Indian and Spanish American workmen, and they added a second story. The walls were not as massive by any means, and it became the living quarters for the commanding officer and his family, after they came out. He occupied it in 1847 and the troops for a time used the lower floor as a barracks. But the kitchen and what was later the dining room on the right hand side of the main hall were retained in their original form.

The flight of stairs went up from the entry hall to the hall on the second floor. The officers also added the pillars, which are such a striking feature in the house even now. It became a southern mansion—as much as he could make it so. And it was a very lovely place. The front of the second floor was a great big sala, sixty feet long. There was a fireplace at either end, and neatly disposed between them and overlooking the front gate was Mary's concert grand Bechstein.

I've been asked by a number of people if Mary herself did any crafts work. And the answer to that is no. Her musical world was a very important one. She played beautifully, she had a charming mezzo soprano voice, she began meeting other people who sang and made music long before the Santa Fe Opera was even a glimpse on the horizon. When I think of Mary I think of music, and then I think of the acequia that ran through the garden below the sala.

There were three bedrooms on the left hand side of the long hall. Mary herself used the back one because it was a corner room and she could have two sides of windows. On the other side of the hall was a study and, I think, storage closets.

Mary had traveled extensively. She had been to Tibet, probably the first American woman to get into that part of the world and actually be presented to the Dalai Lama. She had traveled a great deal in China, Japan, India. She knew the Pacific Islands. She had been to Egypt. I remember a photograph of Mary and her mother, who must have been a demon, taken by the Nile. They went up the Nile in a native boat and saw the pyramids, saw the sphinx. Things that we take for granted in advertising these days had been very real and very wonderful to Mary. She would talk about them when she was in the mood.

Mary came to the Hopi Pueblo once while I was doing research there and we went to the two big dances—the Antelope Dance and the Snake Dance. I had a funny little apartment attached to a guest house, and she and Kenneth Fishee (a curator for the museum of Navajo ceremonial art) came out with a huge basket of Fortnam-Mason food, so that they would be supplied with the kinds of things they were used to, and spent a week out there. We all took our meals out of the hamper. When they left, Mary politely emptied the hamper's contents onto my kitchen shelves.

In all her traveling she had come and gone through London and had been much impressed by Kew Gardens. When she got back to the states—to Boston, which was really her home—she decided that the Boston Indians had done it all right. But since she too was a Bostonian, she was going to do it even more so in New Mexico. So she whittled around with the authorities in Boston and finally came up with a set of blueprints for a formal English garden, which she took in her bag to New Mexico.

I like to think of Mary landing at Lamy with her blueprints. It's a nice human touch. There was just one little thing that slipped up. The blueprints were in English, and the laborers spoke only Spanish. Translating them was a very complicated matter, but it was managed finally by a school teacher.

The garden had running through it (this was very lovely) the acequia madre, which irrigated the whole place. The beds were laid out formally, and there were paths. She planted lilacs—she loved lilacs. By the time I came around (ca. 1956) and lived in that upstairs bedroom for a couple of summers, the garden was a maze of lilacs. They grew up to that second-story gallery. Along the driveway were Linden and Horse Chestnut trees planted alternately, and in the spring when the Horse Chestnut trees bloomed, the candle blossoms sent out a heavenly fragrance along with the lilacs. They all bloomed at the same time.

Those are the things I think of—the music, the little stream running through the garden, the scent of the flowers. It was all very lovely. It was a house where you were as happy inside as out, and that's saying a lot.

There were fine Indian rugs at the Staples ranch, one that Mr. Staples kept for himself. It was forty feet square and had a beautiful, mechanically perfect, design. But Mary didn't offer to buy it. I said, "Mary why didn't you buy it?" She said, "It didn't have orange in it, and you know I love orange. I have to have orange on the floor." And she did. She had this magnificent collection of rugs that are now in the museum. And there is orange in every blessed one.

Mary collected furniture from old houses that had

disintegrated—trasteros, roperos, two or three desks, a very beautiful dining room table—beautiful Spanish colonial furniture. And the daybeds. I can feel those slats yet! She was very conscientious. Every daybed had a hard, firm Simmons mattress that was supposed to cut the shock of the slats, but didn't. There was a goose down cover on top of that, and then pillows and pillows and pillows—all goose down. I don't think anybody now could stand to sleep in that bed, because everyone seems to have an allergy to feathers.

But Los Luceros was a very wonderful place to be. Mary gave you her freedom, and that was about the biggest present anybody could give. It meant a great deal to me. I'll always say that I am one of the few people in the world who will come out bluntly and say "I loved Mary Wheelwright." In spite of her peculiarities. I have my own, God knows. And at Los Luceros it seemed as if a live beauty had been gathered together, all at once. She didn't separate beauty as a part of life. It was life. And that, I think, is the key to Mary Wheelwright.

6

A HOPI WOMAN'S RITUAL

THE HOPIS CAME LATE IN MY LIFE. I had seen Hopi dances at exhibitions, I had admired Hopi textiles and pottery in museums. At the same time, I knew really very little of the life high on the mesas in north central Arizona.

Every anthropologist I have ever known, somewhere along the line, has acquired a group of people whom he referred to as "My Indians." In my own case, naturally, nobody has ever taken the place of the Kiowas. After the Kiowas come the Cheyennes, and the Tewas of the Rio Grande Valley. Then, I think, the Hopis.

We were strangers to begin with. I could talk to any craftsman in any culture, but I could not talk—and I did know how to talk—to Hopi women. Then the Art Museum of Denver sent me out to make recordings of the life of Hopi women. This was Eric Douglas's idea.

"You know very well," he said, "what the percentage of female to male population is in any given group. You know very well, just as I do, that we have a lot of recorded material about the Hopi men. Now, go on, pack your grips and get out into the northern country of the pueblos and make a record of the life of Hopi women."

I went, although packing my grips was not a simple matter, since it entailed packing enough household goods to last me through at least one year and possibly three. As it turned out, three was nearer the case. I had blankets, I had an air mattress, I had pillows, I had linens, I had the requisite minimum of kitchen utensils, and they were all piled with heaps of reference books in the back of one small Plymouth convertible. After it was filled with my belongings it would hold me but seldom any other person.

Finding a place to live in the Hopi country was not easy. The Hopis, as has been said many times by many people, are conservative. They keep themselves to themselves. They are not exactly warmly inclined to strangers. In fact, this latter attitude extends to the point that they don't like to have anybody but

Hopis living around them. In the village where I landed, the newest of the twelve that make up the Hopi communities, there was a trading post and there was a high school. The people who lived in the trading post, and who operated it, were, to the Indians, simply more traders, and they could be accepted on that ground.

Many of the people who were in their middle forties when I got there were educated in Indian service schools and, therefore, schools and schoolteachers were familiar. They would find a room for me, they said, in the accommodations provided for schoolteachers, especially since it was summer and the school was closed for the season. Later, perhaps, I would find other accommodations, and that I ultimately did in the home of a Hopi woman who had built an apartment on the side of her house for her mother. The mother was now deceased, the apartment was vacant, and because the woman had been a schoolteacher herself, she was willing to house me and tuck me away right in the middle of the village.

This, of course, was a blessing in disguise. At the time I looked at it rather dimly, because there was no electricity. All light was by gas or kerosene. There was a well, there was a pump, there was running water. So I could keep myself and my surroundings reasonably clean. But, on the other hand, there was no heat except from a kerosene stove, and I am deadly afraid of kerosene stoves. They have an informal way of going out without entirely extinguishing the flow of gas. So my first lessons in Hopi housekeeping were rugged, as rugged as if I were back in Nambe valley worrying all over again about how to live by myself in simple, if not primitive, surroundings.

The gods were good to me, however, and they sent me another schoolteacher, this one in another village where I would not be accused of spying if I went to visit her, or of sneaking secrets from her or from her husband. I could just come and go as a person, and this was a blessing, as I say, that kept me going and coming for many, many months.

But there were still things to learn. We had been at work for about a month. Alice Bear Woman dictated what she remembered of her girlhood, I scribbled frantically in a stenographer's notebook to get it all down on paper (this was before the days of tape recorders), and watched everything that went on outside the big window that I faced in Alice's kitchen. From there I could see the comings and the goings in the village, the men driving burro trains up the trail, the children running, playing, shouting, often straddling their mother's brooms— imaginary horses. They could not have lived in those remote and high-altitude surroundings without burros, but every Hopi boy yearned frantically, passionately, for the day when a horse might possibly be his. And every imitation of a horse was a treasure to be cherished.

The household where I worked consisted of Alice, her

husband (David Stoneman), their daughter, Renée, and her son, Manuel. Five of us in one kitchen, all of us going about our own business, and each of us only dimly aware of the others unless intruded upon. Then came the day, at the end of the first month, approximately, when Alice said to me quietly (the Hopis are always quiet and soft-voiced), "You don't come to work tomorrow."

"Why not?" I asked. "Is there a dance, is there a ceremony?"

"No, not ceremony," she said thoughtfully, "not exact ceremony, but is woman's ceremony, and you'd better stay home."

"Well," I said, "if it's a woman's ceremony, why can't I be there? Do the men take part in it?"

"No, the mens suffers from it." Alice's eyes began to dance. "Mens suffer bad from this ceremony."

"Well," I said, "if it's a woman's ceremony and the men suffer from it, I think I ought to see it."

"No, you don't see it. You don't come to work tomorrow."

The word had gone forth. I accepted it. What can one do when faced with a determined small Hopi, the top of whose head barely reached the bottom of one's shoulder? So on the following day I stayed home. I cleaned house, I did all of the women's things that I had let go during the month of work. I did some typing, I wrote some letters, I occupied myself. But by four o'clock in the afternoon I was bored. I was used to having company by that time, and Alice and Renée were delightful people to be around, David was very amusing, and I missed them. So on the off chance that the ceremony might have ended before sundown, though I never knew one that did, I got into my battered convertible and drove the twelve miles from one village to another.

The village, when I drove into it, seemed deserted: no children playing in the plaza, no men huskily shouting at their burros, no women grinding corn or spreading corn gruel on their flat cooking stones to make tissue-thin piki bread. Nothing. "Nor sound nor motion" to be detected.

Suddenly the door of a house facing me was flung open and a torrent of women poured out. Their clean, newly ironed housedresses were splattered and caked with mud. They flung their arms heavenward, whether in threat or entreaty I could not tell. And their voices followed the arms, whether praying or cursing I still could not tell.

The first group of women, still wailing, spread out around the plaza, to be followed by a second clutch, who also screamed and who flung handfuls of mud at the firstcomers. Among them I discerned my friends Alice and Renée. They seemed to be the ringleaders. As the women spread around me, Alice clutched my hand and Renée filled my unresisting fist with a handful of rich, squashy mud.

"Come on," Alice urged. "This a mud fight. Every woman got get in it."

Shaking with helpless laughter, I joined in the fray. We drove out fleeing foes across and around the plaza before we clustered in Alice's once-immaculate kitchen to feast. Through the great window we watched the first group of women, armed with mops, buckets, and brooms, enter the house from which they had first run, and start the work of cleaning up.

"Aren't they going to eat?" I inquired.

"When they finish. When new room is clean again."

"Who are they?"

"They the bridegroom's woman kin," Renée informed me from a mouth swollen with piki. "They build that room on his mother's house so young people have a place of their own when they marry."

"Why build a nice new room and then smear it with mud?" I asked

"They don't to smear," Alice said, losing some of her carefully polished government-school English. "We does that."

"But why?"

Alice looked me over and thoughtfully shook her head. "Reason is. . ."

I knew there must be a reason underneath this apparent non-Hopi behavior. After all, the Hopis call themselves the People of Peace. There had to be a reason for warlike action.

"Is because we loves them," Renée said, setting acts in their right perspective. "We don't want some other clan to get them and make them go into that clan's kiva."

In a dim scientific way I could sort out the idea. Children belong to their mother's clans, and the mother's older brothers are responsible for their upbringing. If mother has no brothers, her older male cousins substitute for them. So everybody remains in the same clan, and the father's relationship to his own children remains in the same category as the man who came to dinner, with a gloss of respectability spread over the relationship. Any man has a choice of the kivas he will honor with his presence, or he may be admitted to both. However, the mother and her clan remain the dominants in his life.

"So we has mud fights," Renée continued. "That man's mothers and sisters fix the house up all nice, so that girl will stay in it, and her mothers and sisters go and throw mud in it—all over it, everywheres—so both will get out. And then his folks go in and clean it up."

At that point I discerned through the kitchen window a line of women armed with mops, buckets, and brooms, advancing across the plaza. Their step was deliberate, earth-shaking, and as they passed in front of Alice's window they shook their weapons of cleanliness at us.

"I believe I'll go over and watch them clean up," I murmured.

"Oh, no you don't!" Alice's tone could hardly be classified as a shout, but its meaning was as intense as any that could have been raised. "You belongs to us, now. We take you in. So you gots to stay here, and not go running around strangers. They don't want you." She clutched my hand with a determined paw (blue jeans offer little in the way of handholds) and pulled me down on the bench beside her.

There I sat for the rest of that long summer afternoon. I could see much of what was going on across the plaza. The cleaning must have been thorough, for bucket after bucket of mud was hurled through the door, until the plaza was slippery with it. Only when night began to close over us was I permitted to depart for home, there to write up my field notes for that unbelievable day.

And all the time I was there watching the goings on in the Hopi plaza that afternoon, not a man or a child made an appearance, although I heard their voices clearly from either side of the trail as I drove down from the mesa.

WITH THE HOPIS
IN NEW YORK CITY

T HE INDIAN ARTS AND CRAFTS BOARD of the Department of the Interior (always pronounced as a polysyllable, without intermediate breathing) conditioned almost everybody who came within its sphere. I say <u>almost</u> because there were those few and proud who resisted and maintained their individuality to the end.

Such a one was Fred Kabotie, Hopi artist. Fred came to New York for the opening of the Indian art exhibition at the Museum of Modern Art in 1941, and stayed a month. With him Fred brought, from the New Oraibi High School where he taught, a covey of his students. These young men had worked with him on restoring and reproducing the kiva murals from the prehistoric community of Awatobi, near Keams Canyon, Hopi government headquarters in northeastern Arizona. These living artists were a great addition to a great show. And the Hopis, in uniform red velveteen jackets with silver buttons, red silk (you could buy silk then) scarves tied around their heads, and canaigre-root dyed mid-calf moccasins, also fastened with silver buttons, were beautiful to behold. With them came two or three older men, elders from Fred's home village of Shimopovi to see that none of the young fry, including Fred, got out of line with Hopi standards and rules of behavior. Hopis are Hopis first and human beings afterward, and occasionally the proportions have been known to get out of balance.

Somewhere in the various archives and publications that have grown up out of that last great peace-time display before World War II (and how appropriate to think of the Hopis, the People of Peace, in regard to it) there is a photograph of Eleanor Roosevelt standing with Fred and the others in front of the restored Awatobi murals. Tall, kind, warm Mrs. Roosevelt! Her six feet towered well above Fred's five feet five, but you would never have known that from the picture. Eagerly, patiently, she bent her good ear to catch the words of the quiet desert voices, so whispering in tone compared with the Anglo-American oratory of the Thirties and Forties. What Fred called her "good" smile never left her face, no more than an elfin grin ever left his. Nobody else dared to crack a smile.

That was a few days after the opening. We all felt a little let down and had been frankly afraid that post-excitement depression might overwhelm the Hopis. To the eye they appeared as usual, bland and unperturbed, although a little bored, now that the big push was over. René d'Harnoncourt, our director, summoned me.

"We ought to do something about them Hopis," he began, luxuriating in deliberately misphrasing English words in the Indian fashion.

"Take the rollers away from them?" I flippantly inquired, remembering his early encounter with Ambrose Roan Horse of Fort Wingate School, Fred Kabotie, and the respective Navajo and Hopi Silver Guilds. The Navajos had preferred hammers to the rollers favored by the Hopis to work silver slugs.

"No, I think we let them Hopis keep them rollers," he decided, quoting Ambrose. This was a decision of importance, involving as it did two very different methods of working, each bitterly defended by its users. It stands today. Hopis may use sheet metal and rollers to make jewelry; Navajos must melt down slugs of silver obtained from jewelers, and either cast or hammer the results, doing a lot of hard work to obtain the same results.

"What we gots do," René resumed, "is take them somewheres."

"Where?" I asked, reasonably I hoped.

"You're the only one who has time to do it," he said. "Everybody else is busy. And I thought you might like a change from writing museum labels."

"I would," I said, but hesitated. Experience had taught me that when René held out a flattering piece of bait, there was likely to be a hook somewhere in the background. "Where?" I repeated.

"The Museum of the American Indian."

"Oh." I paused. "It might broaden their horizons," I tentatively agreed, reflecting that it would certainly broaden the soles of my feet to escort the Hopi delegation over that immense acreage of marble floors on Upper Broadway. The Hopis, luckily for them, were already flatfooted.

"I'll talk to Fred," René offered magnanimously, overlooking my unspoken queries and objections. "I'll let you know." He wiggled the bait at the end of his line.

I returned to my typewriter and to hammering out a fair-copy sequence of the captions for the cases. Someone had suggested that the captions might make a foundation for a textbook on Indian Art. They did.

Fred Kabotie sidled through the office door an hour later.

"Boss Man say we go to another museum," he murmured. "Is far?"

"A few miles."

"How we go?"

I was startled. "Why—why—I don't know. I guess we take a cab. How many are going?"

"All of us. Peter and David want to go too."

"Maybe <u>two</u> cabs," I said, mentally calculating the possible displacement.

"Not them trains goes underground? Douglas he tells us 'bout them."

In my mind I consigned Eric Douglas to a place farther underground than even the New York subway had yet penetrated, and took refuge in a woman's last resort. Ten people—all of them strangers to the city's ways—I could not face it! But Fred had his sticking point, too.

"At home we ride in cars. I got big new pickup truck. Cars is nothing new to us."

"Well, you see, these aren't just ordinary cars. They're all painted bright yellow, and they have letters and numbers written all over them."

"We seen them. We ride in them, other day. 'Yellow' they say, but they don't need to. We can see what color they is." Fred was patiently polite, a man addressing a woman to whom he was not related, and for whom he had no established rules of conduct.

"I'll see what Mr. d'Harnoncourt says. Do you want to come with me?"

Together we knocked on the inner office door. René was studying accounts, but he abandoned them instantly. He heard us out.

"You see," he said to Fred, "Miss Marriott comes from outside New York. She's a little timid about some things here that she doesn't see in her home town."

"Timid" precisely described my feelings about the New York subways. Apparently it hit the right note with Fred, too.

"Ladies is like that," he agreed. "Maybe she get over it," he added hopefully. "She oughts to try."

"I'm afraid she won't get over this," René said, gently— gentle to my foolishness, gentle to Fred's disappointment. "Ladies have a hard time. . . "

In a sudden flash, a compromise presented itself. "Why not go up on the bus?" I asked. "We can see lots more than if we went underground, or even in a cab. The top deck of a bus. . ."

René bestowed on me his "You really are brighter than I thought" expression and nodded approvingly.

"Why don't you go that way?" he agreed. "Fred, how would you like that?"

"Climb up there and ride on it like a rodeo horse?" Fred reflected. "Maybeso. I never rode no horse, just a burro. But one time I ride bicycle." His face lit up in that all-encompassing grin that was completely part of Fred. "Dr. Hewett—he the archaeologist—you know, well, he say three us boys was going to work for him on summer dig could ride from Santa Fe to Jemez Springs on bicycles. Was haaaard trip. One boy give out, but us other two kept on going: through Sandía, Santa Ana, Zía, going, going to Jemez Hot Springs. We get punctures till we has to ride on rims, we get hungry, and the people in them down-river pueblos feeds us. We don't see <u>no</u> white people till we get to Jemez and Dr. Hewett come out to meet us." He stopped. He had reached the climax and conclusion of his narrative simultaneously.

"Bus be good," Fred said decisively, and walked out.

"I wonder," René mused, "if the bus reminds him of the bicycle? Maybe that's why it's good."

"Or it may fulfill a suppressed desire to ride a horse?" I suggested. "What do we do first?"

"Pass the word around," René said.

"Oh, that's already taken care of," I replied.

"Good old moccasins telegraph. All right. Hoist them aboard in the morning." He groped in his pocket and came up with two crumpled twenty dollar bills. It has always puzzled me why a man so fastidious in every other way could have tolerated money that could only be described as maculate. "Here. This ought to pay the bus fare and buy some lunch for all of you."

"I was going to pay for the trip," I protested.

"No doubt," said René judicially. "It will probably be worth whatever it could cost you. On the other hand, no. I shall do penance by lunching with the Board, and I want to think I have provided some happiness for someone on an otherwise gloomy day."

"Gee, t'anks, Boss," I muttered and departed in a cloud of Erle Stanley Gardner, my current soporific.

In the morning, Fred and his cohorts and I gathered in front of the museum at nine o'clock, our usual going-to-work time. The Hopis would have preferred an earlier time, and said so, but with more presence of mind than I would have given myself credit for, I pointed out that the sun had to top the tall buildings for its light to penetrate the canyons. We walked the half-block to 54th street amicably.

It was a heavenly day. When I think back on that winter, I think in the grimmest grimiest tones of the Ash Can School of Art, with only a few flashes of bright color. This was one of the brilliant times.

Going uptown on the double-decker bus, with the sun's rays shooting before us from the right, everything was clear and bright in color; everything had sharpened tones. Our deck was enclosed, but we saw much, and whenever the vehicle lurched around a corner, we held our collective breath, waiting for the next wave of buildings to engulf us. Nobody said anything.

We reached Broadway and 155th street. A marble plaza opened before us, framed on three sides by marble buildings. I led the way down the spiral stairs of the bus, then across the plaza to the building on the southern side. It was familiar, but I would never be quite at ease with it however much I worked with its collections.

We were expected. We pushed a quite ordinary doorbell, and the door was opened to us. We stepped inside, rubbed our feet on the mat, and crossed the marble floor to the elevator, which lumbered complainingly upward to the third floor. More marble. The Curator of North American Indian Art awaited us.

The Museum of the American Indian, Heye Foundation, or "The Heye" as it was known in the profession, was in those days a very different place from today's "Indian Museum." Mr. George Heye, founder, financier, President of the Board, and pack-rat collector was alive and in control. Mrs. Heye had wanted a representative collection. He wanted everything any Indian anywhere might have owned, used, needed or wanted. To house all this he had constructed the museum on upper Broadway on land he shared with the Hispanic Society, the National Geographic, and the Daughters of the American Revolution. This somewhat incongruous combination of uplift and education existed in apparent harmony by the simple device of never crossing one another's thresholds. When Mr. Heye's space on Upper Broadway was filled, he simply constructed what he by choice and the rest of the world by necessity called "the Annex" on Van Cortlandt Park, in the Bronx.

But it was the main collection and its displays that

concerned the Hopis, and they promptly took off their coats, hung them on chairs, and proceeded to investigate quietly, politely, and thoroughly.

The Navajo and Plains displays concerned them little. "Just like Flagstaff powwow on the Fourth of July" was their summing up and dismissal. Fine quillwork, beadwork, birchbark inlay, fabric applique, and combinations of two or more elements from the Great Lakes tribes were more interesting because of their intricacies.

The Eskimos got passing marks. "They looks like peoples. Got real Hopi faces. How they sound when they talk?" At that time the curator and I decided it was time for lunch, and we all adjourned to a nearby cafeteria. To my relief and the Hopis' joy there was mutton on the steam table—"cooked to cat's meat," my English grandmother would have said, but also cooked to a proper Hopi degree of doneness. Whispers of joyful anticipation greeted the welcome sight.

"Do they eat *THAT*?" the curator exclaimed.

"At home they'd eat everything but the wool and the claw," I replied loftily. The Hopi did indeed eat the mutton, and went back for seconds. Apparently they had finally found something in this strange new world with which they felt completely at home. The curator was as fascinated as I was. He insisted on paying for the lunch, although I assured him that the original intention had been to have him as our guest.

The afternoon passed pleasantly, in familiar surroundings. We concentrated on Hopi and other Pueblo displays, which were "right" to put in a museum. The older men explained to Fred, who explained to me, who tried to explain to the curator, the meanings of some designs. Over the pottery from the prehistoric Mimbres culture of southwestern New Mexico, Fred spent a long time, carefully studying it, bowl by bowl.

"Looks like Hopi someways," he observed. Then, with a lifting of his head, "You think they was maybe old time Hopis? Them pictures could have Hopi meanings." None of us could see forty years ahead, to the publication of his book on Hopi interpretations of Mimbres designs [*Designs from the Ancient Membrenos with a Hopi Interpretation* (San Francisco: Grabhorn Press, 1949)].

It was time to go. As we walked back to the bus stop, with warm farewells and thanks on both sides still in our ears, the sun was slanting across the street in the opposite direction from that of the morning, but still from our right. We passed a store we had not noticed in the morning, although its red-and-gold decorations were designed to catch the eye.

"What's that place?" Fred demanded, halting to point with his pursed lips.

"A cigar store. Didn't you see it coming up?"

"No. Why they got Geronimo standing out there in front?"

"It wasn't meant to be Geronimo, but Sitting Bull." I was getting tired—too tired to argue. "People see him, they know Indians discover tobacco, they come in. Buy." I'm talking like a Hopi myself, I thought in bewilderment.

"Got watches, too. Loooots watches."

Indeed, there was a card full of bright, enamel-rimmed wrist watches in the window. "Come on," Fred directed. "We go buy watch." He summoned his attendants with a jerk of his head, and we all trooped into the store.

Buying the watches seemed to be an endless business. One watch cost so much, four watches bought together meant a lower unit price, and all twelve watches on the card could be bought for as much as eleven units. Hopis are shrewd and canny traders and they never, in their own world, have need for haste. Buying the one card of twelve took over an hour. When the business deal was completed, the watches paid for, and we were outside again, Fred turned to me.

"I guess we take the cab back. You look tired."

I was, and sank beside him on the seat of the first of the three cabs we commandeered. Fred opened his package and examined its contents.

"Pretty." He held up a blue-rimmed watch. "Is right color for my mother's brother. My old uncle."

Methodically, he went through the watches, one at a time, deciding which of his clan uncles and brothers should have what watch. He laid them out along the sleeve of his coat to determine specific ceremonial colors. At last all was decided, with one watch left over. We had reached 57th street by this time, even with late afternoon traffic.

"Here," Fred held the remaining watch out to me. "You take it."

"Why?" I asked bewildered.

"You good to us. We all have nice day together, with you and that man. You treat us good." Then, with purest pragmatism, "Is green. Got no clan color green. You wear green lots times. So is good color for you. If I take back one watch wrong color, everybody think is funny and nobody want wrong watch. They laugh at me. This way they never see it, nobody tells them, you got pretty watch, everybody happy. And it don't cost nothing. Is free watch on card."

The cab stopped before the Museum of Modern Art and we all emerged, I with my new free green watch, which I still have, the Hopis with their own memories of that special day at The Heye.

EDITOR'S ANNOTATIONS

Despite her advanced age and frail physical condition at the time these memoirs were recorded and transcribed, Alice Marriott was remarkably accurate in relating her memories of the important people and events in her life. The following annotations simply add a few more details and information the editor feels might be of interest to the reader.

Margaret Lefranc (Frankel) Schoonover (1907–1998), a color expressionist who worked with oil, graphics, and all watercolor media, illustrated a number of Alice Marriott's books. She and Alice shared the primitive adobe house in Nambe in the forties while Alice was doing her research for *Maria: The Potter of San Ildefonso.* That classic volume, still in print, won the 1948 Fifty Best Books of the Year Illustration award. The Library of Congress's One Hundred Best Books of the Year award was given to the Lefranc illustrated *Indians of the Four Corners* (1952) and *The Valley Below* (1949), the latter a delightful account of the day-to-day challenges experienced by the two women while living in Nambe. Margaret's oils and watercolors appeared in important exhibitions in the United States and France.

L-R: Margaret Lefranc Schoonover, Maria Martinez, and Alice Marriott at a Book-Signing Event for *Maria: The Potter of San Ildefonso.* Courtesy University of Oklahoma, Norman, Oklahoma, ca. 1948, Photo #578

After moving around the world for a good part of her life, Margaret Lefranc Schoonover settled in Santa Fe, where she designed and built a charming adobe house, doing all but the heaviest construction herself. About the same time, she bought and restored an old home in Coconut Grove, Miami. She would divide her time between the two cities, driving or flying (with her beloved cat Winter) twice a year to escape the weather extremes in each city.

It was on one of those cross-country trips, in 1972, that I first met Margaret Lefranc Schoonover. She and her friend Sandra Edelman stopped by the Southern Methodist University's editorial office of the *Southwest Review*, where I was working with legendary editor Margaret L. Hartley (1909–1983). From that first meeting a long and productive friendship developed. Margaret and Winter would stay at our home in Dallas on her trips back and forth (Winter was not up to traveling the whole distance from Miami to Santa Fe all at once). Thanks to Margaret we were introduced to Alice Marriott and she would be very pleased that with this volume Alice's memoirs are being given the recognition they deserve.

René d'Harnoncourt (1901–1968), another of Alice's longtime friends and mentors, had assembled an impressive collection of folk art while he was in Mexico (1925–1927), ten years before he met Alice. He rose to prominence in 1930, after the Metropolitan Museum of Art featured an exhibition of his collection. After his marriage in 1932 to Chicago fashion designer Sara Carr, he hosted his own radio show, "Art in America (1933– 1934)," and taught at Sara Lawrence College and the New School for Social Research (1934–1937). He and Alice met in 1936, when he was appointed administrator for the Indian Arts and Crafts Board. During his tenure he mounted one of the first national exhibitions of Native American arts at the Golden Gate International Exposition in San Francisco in 1939. Beginning in 1944, René d'Harnoncourt sensitively and successfully filled the roles of Curator and Director of New York's Museum of Modern Art. He retired from that distinguished career in 1968. His life ended tragically that same year. While walking near his home on Long Island, he was struck and killed by a drunken driver.

John Collier (1901–1980) was another of Alice Marriott's favorites. In 1933 he wrote "A Bill of Rights for the Indians," a moving account of the disgraceful way the United States treated its native people for almost three hundred years. As Commissioner of Indian Affairs during the first Franklin Roosevelt Administration, Collier was instrumental in winning congressional backing for the Indian Reorganization Act of 1934. This legislation dramatically changed United States government policy toward American Indians by allowing tribal self-government and consolidating individual land allotments back into tribal hands.

British-born John Collier was also a poet, author, and screenplay writer. Many of his short stories appeared in *The New Yorker* during the thirties, forties, and fifties.

Two of the "do-gooders" recognized by Alice Marriott were Dwight Whitney Morrow (1873–1931) and his wife Elizabeth Reeve Cutter Morrow (1873–1955), parents of the famous Anne Morrow Lindbergh (1906–2001). The Morrows, great philanthropists and volunteers for worthy causes, supported the work of Alice Marriott and others in their efforts to improve the lives of the American Indian. Dwight Morrow was appointed ambassador to Mexico by President Calvin Coolidge from 1927 to 1930. Later he became U. S. Senator from New Jersey. Elizabeth was active in promoting women's education and served as acting president of her alma mater Smith College. She supervised a household that fostered achievement.

Throughout her memoirs Alice Marriott mentions the contributions of the "first Mrs. Ickes," who was Anna Wilmarth Thompson Ickes. Harold Ickes (1874–1952) married Anna in 1911. He served as Secretary of the Interior from 1933 to 1946, appointed to that position by President Franklin Delano Roosevelt. Under FDR he helped implement the national "New Deal" program. Anna died in an automobile accident in 1935. The second Mrs. Ickes was Jane Dahlman Ickes, whom Harold married in 1938 when he was sixty-four and she twenty-five.

When describing the ingenuity of the Navajo and Apaches in developing metalworking techniques, Alice Marriott tells of the Long Walk to the Bosque Redondo in the early 1860s. This was a forced march (organized by Kit Carson) of 8,500 Navajo men, women, and children who were herded for almost four hundred miles to a desolate forty-square-mile tract of land on the Pecos River in New Mexico. The Bosque Redondo reservation had poor water, a minimal supply of firewood, and was already occupied by Mescalero Apaches. Hundreds of Navajos, including women and children, died traveling in harsh winter conditions for almost two months. The plan of the United States government, which ultimately failed miserably, was to turn the Indians into farmers and "civilize" them by sending them to school and forcing them to accept and practice Christian beliefs. Finally recognizing that the Indian removal effort was poorly planned and a total failure, the United States Treaty of 1868 allowed the Navajo to return to their former, although greatly reduced, territory along the Arizona-New Mexico border, where they developed the largest Native American community in the United States.

Frederic (Eric) H. Douglas (1897–1956), whom Alice Marriott describes as "one of the great men who lived and breathed and worked and talked . . . in the Indian field," made important and innovative changes in the methods used to exhibit the art of Native Americans. From the time he was with the Denver Art Museum as Curator of Indian Art Douglas sought to take a fresh and universal approach to the subject of art and Native American peoples. He focused on the aesthetic properties of the works rather than their significance as ethnographic or anthropological specimens. During his long tenure with the Denver Art Museum (1929–1956), Douglas became involved with all the major exhibitions of American Indian art in the United States, including the Exposition of Indian Tribal Arts (1939 World's Fair in San Francisco). In 1941 the Museum of Modern Art asked Douglas to design an "Indian Art of the United States" exhibition. Considered revolutionary at the time, Douglas's approach to exhibiting Indian art has become today's standard.

Mabel Morrow, a colleague of Alice Marriott's at the Sherman Institute, is the author of *Indian Rawhide: An American Folk Art* (Norman: University of Oklahoma Press, 1975). Morrow's book is a definitive study and primary resource on the unique American Indian art form of parfleche (treated rawhide) production, with drawings and paintings by the author and a foreword by Alice Marriott. In the twenties and thirties, while she was a teacher with the Bureau of Indian Affairs in South

Dakota, Mabel Morrow collected cutout silhouettes. These Native American patterns—usually depicting flora and fauna near their reservations—were cut from birch bark and used to decorate clothing, canoes, pots, tools, and note cards among other things. The Morrow cutout collection is housed today in the Museum of International Folk Art in Santa Fe, New Mexico.

Kenneth Milton Chapman (1875–1968), another colleague of Alice's at the Sherman Institute, was an educator and artist who studied the techniques of Indian handicrafts. Chapman was discovered by Edgar Hewett, who found a position for him in the Art Department at New Mexico Normal University (now New Mexico Highlands University) in Las Vegas, New Mexico.

Dr. Edgar Lee Hewett (1865–1946), senior member of the Sherman Institute faculty in 1938, is well known for initiating the Antiquities Act, one of the most important pieces of legislature for the conservation movement in the United States.

Dr. Hewett was the founder and first director of the Museum of New Mexico and the first president of New Mexico Normal School. His association with Maria Martinez made San Ildefonso Pueblo a center for Native American pottery. Hewett also had a significant role in the formation of Bandelier National Monument and Chaco Culture National Historical Park.

Alice Marriott refers to Bruns Hospital in Santa Fe as an "army reclamation project." The hospital was opened in 1942 as Bruns General Army Hospital and served as a recovery center for survivors of the Bataan Death March. It was also a Japanese Internment camp. After World War II the hospital was acquired by the Christian Brothers and became St. Michael's College (today the College of Santa Fe).

Alice's friend Mabel Evans Dodge Sterne Luhan, née Ganson (1879–1962), a wealthy American patron of the arts, wrote her autobiography *Intimate Memories* in 1933. In it she detailed her full life with four husbands and a number of lovers, both male and female. She married Carl Evans in 1900 and became a widow two and a half years later following his death in a hunting accident. Her second marriage, in 1903, to wealthy architect Edwin Dodge, ended in divorce in 1916 after her stormy relationship with Jack Reed. Refusing Reed's marriage proposal, Mabel instead took Maurice Sterne, a painter, as her third husband. But Sterne was no match for Tony Luhan, the determined native American who wanted her as his wife. Tony set up a teepee in front of her Taos home and drummed each night till Mabel came to him. After her brief but famous encounter with D. H. Lawrence, Mabel married Tony Luhan in 1923, a union that lasted, perhaps surprisingly, until her death.

Oliver La Farge (1901–1963) was another of Alice's distinguished friends. An American writer and anthropologist who spent much of his life championing Indian rights, La Farge won the 1930 Pulitzer Prize for *Laughing Boy: A Navajo Love Story*. The book focuses on the clash of Anglo and Native American cultures during the second decade of the twentieth century.

It was through Mary Cabot Wheelwright (1878–1958) that Alice Marriott met a number of interesting people, including famous coloratura soprano Lily Pons (1898–1976), American Indian and landscape photographer Laura Gilpin (1891–1979), and British socialite Dorothy Brett (1883–1977), who painted portraits of English celebrities, including novelist D. H. Lawrence.

Lily Pons came to the United States from France in 1931 and made her Metropolitan Opera debut as Lucia in Donizetti's *Lucia di Lammermoor*. Her flawless technique, perfect pitch (she could reach A-flat above high C), and attractive appearance contributed to her success. She was a principal soprano at the Met for almost thirty years (1931–1960). Her marriage of twenty years to conductor André Kostelanetz ended in 1958.

Laura Gilpin's splendid black-and-white photographs of southwestern landscapes, many of which were peopled with

Navajo and Pueblo Indians, have become treasured collectibles. She considered exceptionally fine landscapes difficult to find and photograph, but she welcomed the challenge. Just weeks before her death at the age of eighty-eight she was taking her last photographs from the window of a small plane flying low over the Rio Grande.

In 1924, Dorothy Eugenie Brett came to Taos from England, where she had enjoyed a life of wealth and privilege as the daughter of a close advisor to Queen Victoria. Among the British notables painted by The Honorable Dorothy Brett were D. H. Lawrence and his wife Frieda. Brett joined the Lawrences when they came to Taos at the invitation of Mabel Dodge Luhan. The Lawrences moved on, but Dorothy Brett stayed, becoming a naturalized citizen in 1938 and a permanent artist/writer in residence. Brett became deaf at the age of twenty-seven and for the rest of her life she carried a brass ear trumpet, a long contraption slotted at the end, which contributed to her reputation as one of the eccentric characters in the Taos community.

These and dozens of other creative, independent men and women gravitated to Santa Fe and Taos in the thirties and forties, many encouraged to visit the primitive high desert by Mary Wheelwright. Mary herself was born into a wealthy Boston family, but rather than settle into the comfortable life of pampered socialite, she traveled extensively and developed an interest in the history of religions. She found a focus for her energies when she came to New Mexico in the twenties and met Hastiin Klah (1867-1937), an esteemed Navajo singer and a medicine man, who was attempting to preserve ritual religious practices of the Navajos. Wheelwright and Klah collaborated in the creation of a permanent record of great Navajo narratives. Mary concentrated on recording Klah's memories of the spoken word in Navajo ritual. Klah, who was also a skilled weaver, produced huge tapestries that became permanent records of the sand paintings, which traditionally were created and destroyed during Navajo healing ceremonies. To preserve the collected sound recordings, manuscripts, paintings, and sand painting tapestries, Mary decided that a permanent repository would be necessary in order to show the public the beauty, dignity, and profound logic of Navajo religion. She called in architect William Penhallow Henderson, who based his design for the museum on the hooghan, the traditional Navajo home and the setting for Navajo ceremonies. Klah blessed the building site, but he died a few months before the museum was completed. First called the Navajo House of Prayer and House of Navajo Religion, the facility officially became the Museum of Navajo Ceremonial Art in the thirties. Today it is the much visited Wheelwright Museum of the American Indian in Santa Fe.

BOOKS BY ALICE MARRIOTT

The Ten Grandmothers. Norman: University of Oklahoma Press, 1945.

Winter Telling Stories. New York: William Sloan Associates, Incorporated, 1947.

Indians on Horseback. New York: Thomas Y. Crowell, 1948.

Maria: The Potter of San Ildefonso. Norman: University of Oklahoma Press, 1948.

The Valley Below. Norman: University of Oklahoma Press, 1949.

These Are the People: Some Notes on the Southwestern Indians. Santa Fe: Laboratory of Anthropology, 1949.

Indians of the Four Corners: The Anasazi and Their Pueblo Descendants. New York: Thomas Y. Crowell, 1952.

Greener Fields: Experiences among the American Indians. New York: Thomas Y. Crowell, 1953. [first published 1952.]

Hell on Horses and Women: Norman: University of Oklahoma Press, 1953.

Sequoyah: Leader of the Cherokees. New York: Random House, 1956.

The Black Stone Knife. New York: Thomas Y. Crowell, 1957.

The First Comers: Indians of America's Dawn. New York: David McKay Company, 1960.

Indian Annie: Kiowa Captive. New York: David McKay Company, 1965

Kiowa Year: A Study in Culture Impact. New York: The Macmillan Company, 1967.

BOOKS BY ALICE MARRIOTT AND CAROL K. RACHLIN

American Indian Mythology. New York: Thomas Y. Crowell, 1968.

Saynday's People: The Kiowa People and the Stories They Told. Lincoln: University of Nebraska Press, 1963. [This book combines *Winter-Telling Stories* and *Indians on Horseback.*]

American Epic: The Story of the American Indian. New York: G. P. Putnam's Sons, 1969.

Peyote: An Account of the Origins and Growth of the Peyote Religion. New York: Thomas Y. Crowell, 1971.

Oklahoma: The Forty-Sixth Star. Garden City, New York: Doubleday, 1973.

Plains Indian Mythology. New York: Thomas Y. Crowell, 1975.

Dance Around the Sun. New York: Thomas Y. Crowell, 1977.

LaVergne, TN USA
16 May 2010
182878LV00002B/34/P